Pre-GED Connection™

Language Arts, Reading

**by Marilyn Shepard
and Ann Greenberger**

LiteracyLink® is a joint project of PBS,
Kentucky Educational Television,
the National Center on Adult Literacy,
and the Kentucky Department of Education.

This project is funded in whole,
or in part, by the Star Schools Program
of the USDE under contract #R203D60001.

Reading Level:	**6 - 8**
Category:	**GED Material**
Subcategory:	**GED–Reading**
Workbook Available:	
Teacher Guide Available:	
Part of a Series:	**Yes**
CD / CD ROM / DVD Available:	**Yes**

 PBS LiteracyLink®

 KET

 NCAL

Acknowledgments

LiteracyLink® Advisory Board
Lynn Allen, Idaho Public Television
Anthony Buttino, WNED-TV
Anthony Carnevale, Educational
    Testing Service
Andy Chaves, Marriott International, Inc.
Patricia Edwards, Michigan State University
Phyllis Eisen, Center for Workforce Success National
    Association of Manufacturers
Maggi Gaines, Baltimore Reads, Inc.
Marshall Goldberg, Association of Joint Labor
    Management Educational Programs
Milton Goldberg, National Alliance
    for Business
Neal Johnson, Association of Governing Boards of
    Universities and Colleges
Cynthia Johnston, Central Piedmont Community
    College
Sandra Kestner, Kentucky Department for Adult
    Education and Literacy
Thomas Kinney, American Association of Adult and
    Continuing Education
Dale Lipschultz, American Library Association
Lennox McLendon, National Adult Education
    Professional Development Consortium
Cam Messina, KLRN
Patricia Miller, KNPB
Cathy Powers, WLRN
Ray Ramirez, U.S. Department of Education
Emma Rhodes, (retired) Arkansas Department of
    Education
Cynthia Ruiz, KCET
Tony Sarmiento, Worker Centered Learning,
    Working for America Institute
Steve Steurer, Correctional
    Education Association
LaShell Stevens-Staley, Iowa PTV
Fran Tracy-Mumford, Delaware Department of
    Adult/Community Education
Terilyn Turner, Community Education,
    St. Paul Public Schools

LiteracyLink®
Ex Officio Advisory Board
Joan Auchter, GED Testing Service
Barbara Derwart, U.S. Department of Labor
Cheryl Garnette, OERI, U.S.
    Department of Education
Andrew Hartman, National Institute
    for Literacy
Mary Lovell, OVAE, U.S. Department
    of Education
Ronald Pugsley, OVAE, U.S. Department
    of Education
Linda Roberts, U.S. Department of Education
Joe Wilkes, OERI, U.S. Department of Education

LiteracyLink® Partners
LiteracyLink® is a joint project of:
    Public Broadcasting Service,
    Kentucky Educational Television,
    National Center on Adult Literacy, and the
    Kentucky Department of Education.

Content Design and Workbook
Editorial Development
    Learning Unlimited, Oak Park, Illinois
Design and Layout
    By Design, Lexington, Kentucky
Project Coordinators
    Milli Fazey, KET, Lexington, Kentucky
    Margaret Norman, KET, Lexington, Kentucky

This project is funded in whole, or in part, by the
Star Schools Program of the USDE under contract
#R203D60001.

PBS LiteracyLink® is a registered mark of the
Public Broadcasting Service.

Contents

Introduction

Welcome to *Pre-GED Language Arts, Reading*. This workbook is part of the *LiteracyLink®* multimedia educational system for adult learners and educators. The system includes *Pre-GED Connection*, which builds a foundation for GED-level study and *GED Connection*, which learners use to study for the GED Tests. *LiteracyLink* also includes *Workplace Essential Skills*, which targets upgrading the knowledge and skills needed to succeed in the world of work.

Pre-GED CONNECTION
consists of these educational tools:

26 VIDEO PROGRAMS shown
on public television and in
adult learning centers

ONLINE MATERIALS available
on the Internet at
http://www.pbs.org/literacy

FIVE Pre-GED COMPANION
WORKBOOKS
Language Arts, Writing
Language Arts, Reading
Social Studies
Science
Mathematics

Instructional Programs

Pre-GED Connection consists of 26 instructional video programs and five companion workbooks. Each *Pre-GED Connection* workbook lesson accompanies a video program. For example, the first lesson in this book is *Program 7— Nonfiction*. This workbook lesson should be used with *Pre-GED Connection Video Program 7— Nonfiction*. In addition, you can go online to www.pbs.org/literacy and click the *Pre-GED Reading* link.

Who's Responsible for LiteracyLink®?

LiteracyLink was developed through a five-year grant by the U.S. Department of Education. The following partners have contributed to the development of the *LiteracyLink* system:

| PBS Adult Learning Service | Kentucky Educational Television (KET) | The National Center on Adult Literacy (NCAL) of the University of Pennsylvania | The Kentucky Department of Education |

All of the *LiteracyLink* partners wish you the very best in meeting all of your educational goals.

Before you start using the workbook, take some time to preview its features.

1. Take the **Pretest** on page 2. This will help you decide on which areas you need to focus. You should use the evaluation chart on page 13 to develop your study plan.

2. Work through the **workbook lessons**—each one corresponds to a video program.

   The *Before You Watch* feature sets up the video program:
   - **Think About the Topic** gives a brief overview of the video
   - **Prepare to Watch the Video** is a short activity with instant feedback that shows how everyday knowledge can help you better understand the topic
   - **Lesson Goals** highlight the main ideas of each video and workbook lesson
   - **Terms** introduces key reading vocabulary

   The *After You Watch* feature helps you evaluate what you have just seen in the program:

   - **Think About the Program** presents questions that focus on key points from the video
   - **Make the Connection** applies what you have learned to real-life situations

   Three *Reading Skills* sections correspond to key concepts in the video program.

   The *GED Test Taking Skill* sections introduce you to GED-style questions and to special features of the GED Reading Test.

   The *Reading Writing Connection* sections offer you an opportunity to use what you are reading to help develop your writing skills, two activities that often go hand in hand.

   GED Practice allows you to practice with the types of problems that you will see on the actual test.

3. Take the **Posttest** on page 94 to determine your progress and whether you are ready for GED-level work.

4. Use the **Answer Key** to check your answers.

5. Refer to the **Reading Resources** at the back of the book as needed.

For Teachers

Portions of *LiteracyLink* have been developed for adult educators and service providers. Teachers can use Pre-GED lesson plans in the ***LiteracyLink Teacher's Guide*** binder. This binder also contains lesson plans for ***GED Connection*** and ***Workplace Essential Skills***.

Reading Pretest

The Reading Pretest on the following pages is similar to the GED Reading Tests. However, it has only 20 items, compared with 40 items on the actual GED Reading Test. This pretest consists of short nonfiction, fiction, poetry, and drama passages. Each passage is preceded by a "purpose question." This is not the title of the selection; rather, it is a question intended to guide your reading of the piece. You should think about the purpose question as you read the selection.

Read the purpose question, read the selection, and answer the multiple-choice questions. You may refer back to the passage whenever you wish.

The purpose of the Pretest is to evaluate your skills with reading selections and answering questions based on them. Do not worry if you cannot answer every question or if you get some questions wrong. The Pretest will help you identify the types of reading materials and skills that you need to work on.

Directions

1. Read the sample passage and test item on page 3 to become familiar with the test format.

2. Take the test on pages 4 through 11. Read each passage, and then choose the best answer to each question.

3. Record your answers on the answer sheet below, using a No. 2 pencil.

4. Check your work against the Answers and Explanations on page 12.

5. Enter your scores in the evaluation chart on page 13.

READING PRETEST ■ ANSWER SHEET

Name _____   Date _____

Class _____

1. ①②③④⑤	6. ①②③④⑤	11. ①②③④⑤	16. ①②③④⑤
2. ①②③④⑤	7. ①②③④⑤	12. ①②③④⑤	17. ①②③④⑤
3. ①②③④⑤	8. ①②③④⑤	13. ①②③④⑤	18. ①②③④⑤
4. ①②③④⑤	9. ①②③④⑤	14. ①②③④⑤	19. ①②③④⑤
5. ①②③④⑤	10. ①②③④⑤	15. ①②③④⑤	20. ①②③④⑤

Sample Passage and Test Item

The following passage and test item are similar to those you will find on the Reading Pretest. Read the purpose question, the short passage, and the test item. Then go over the sample answer sheet and explanation of why the correct answer is correct.

<u>Question 0</u> refers to the following passage.

ARE YOU ALLERGIC TO CATS?

You probably know someone who is allergic to cats. Even without coming into contact with a cat, people with allergies to cats can sneeze and become congested and cough. This is because cat dander is everywhere a cat has been—the couch, the dining room, the carpet, the bed. The material that people are allergic to is actually in the cat's saliva. Cats groom themselves with their tongues, and the saliva dries on the cat hair. This dander is sticky and lightweight. It adheres to everything—walls, furniture, clothing. In fact, this material is so determined to hang around that it takes six months after a cat is gone for most of the allergen to go away.

0. Which of the following statements best summarizes the main idea of the passage?

   (1) Getting rid of cat allergies is easy if you know what to do.
   (2) It's important to be patient with people who have cat allergies.
   (3) Cleaning your house ensures that visitors will not have an allergic reaction to cats.
   (4) Allergens are tricky to get rid of and are everywhere your cat has been.
   (5) More research is needed to figure out why people are allergic to cats.

Marking the Answer Sheet

0. ①②③④⑤

The correct answer is **(4) Allergens are tricky to get rid of and are everywhere your cat has been.** Therefore, answer space 4 is marked on the answer sheet, as shown above. The space should be filled in completely using a No. 2 pencil. If you change your mind about an answer, erase it completely.

Answer and Explanation

0. **(4) Allergens are tricky to get rid of and are everywhere your cat has been.** (Comprehension) This answer is correct because the details support this option. For example, one detail in the passage is that the dander is sticky and adheres to everything. Another detail says dander can be found six months after the cat has been removed.

Reading Pretest

Choose the <u>one best answer</u> to the questions below.

<u>Questions 1 through 5</u> are based on the nonfiction passage below.

DID THIS BOY MAKE THE BASKETBALL TEAM?

I remember vividly the last time I cried. I was twelve years old, in the seventh grade, and I had tried out for the junior high school basketball team.

5 I walked into the gymnasium; there was a piece of paper tacked to the bulletin board.

It was a cut list. The seventh grade coach had put it up on the board. The
10 boys whose names were on the list were still on the team; they were welcome to keep coming to practices. The boys whose names were not on the list had been cut; their presence
15 was no longer desired. My name was not on the list.

I had not known the cut was coming that day. I stood and I stared at the list. The coach had not composed it
20 with a great deal of subtlety; the names of the very best athletes were at the top of the sheet of paper, and the other members of the squad were listed in what appeared to be a
25 descending order of talent. I kept looking at the bottom of the list, hoping against hope that my name would miraculously appear there if I looked hard enough.

30 I held myself together as I walked out of the gym and out of the school, but when I got home I began to sob. I couldn't stop. For the first time in my life, I had been told officially that I
35 wasn't good enough.

From *Cut*
By Bob Greene

1. Which of the following statements best expresses the main idea?
   (1) The last time he cried, Greene was twelve years old.
   (2) If he'd known the cut was that day, Greene wouldn't have cried.
   (3) The coach needed better skills for dealing with the cut list.
   (4) Greene had a lot of hope that his name would appear on the list.
   (5) This was the first time Greene experienced not being good enough.

2. What is the purpose of the details in paragraph 3?

   The details show that Greene
   (1) thought he'd be on the team
   (2) knew he wasn't a good player
   (3) was angry good players were first
   (4) didn't have self-confidence
   (5) was surprised and unprepared

3. What advice would the author most likely give to his child about trying out for a sports team?
   (1) Always push yourself to be the best athlete you can be.
   (2) It is good to be tough when it comes to school sports.
   (3) You're a worthwhile person, no matter what happens.
   (4) If you are going to cry, don't do it in front of others.
   (5) Keep in mind that coaches can be insensitive.

4. What is the effect of the first sentence, "I remember vividly the last time I cried"?
   (1) It shows that nothing sad has happened to him since then.
   (2) It shows he doesn't believe in crying now.
   (3) It shows he has had a lot of success in his life.
   (4) It sets up an emotionally important story.
   (5) It shows he has a good memory.

5. In another essay, this author writes about an unwed mother who drops out of high school but graduates twenty years later. Based on this and the passage, which of the following best describes the essays by this author?
   (1) sad but heartwarming stories
   (2) uplifting from start to finish
   (3) elaborate and emotionally complex
   (4) unsentimental and technical
   (5) overly dramatic

Questions 6 through 10 are based on the fiction passage below

WHAT IS THIS GIRL EXCITED ABOUT?

To the adult eye it was just the prosaic and none-too-tidy arcade leading into Madison Square Garden. But to the bright-eyed little girl of seven
5 bounding up the slight incline with her uncle, the doors ahead of them were gateways to magic portals to never-never land. She had never been to a circus before and for two weeks now
10 (ever since her uncle had told her) the anticipation of it had tinted her days with an unreal glow, and peopled her nights with motley visitors of fancy.

Oh, why does he walk so slowly? she
15 thought; how could this tall, usually playful uncle of hers be so deliberate? She began tugging at his sleeve, urging him forward, and he glanced down at her and gently smiled. Then he clasped
20 her eager little hand as a side current in the throng threatened to separate them. But he did not quicken his steps and it seemed an hour to Helen before they reached the red-faced
25 guard who performed the magic ritual of ripping their tickets in half and returning the stubs, thereby permitting them to pass through the gate.

From *Part of the Act*
By Sidney Alexander

6. Which of the following happened first in the second paragraph?
   (1) The guard ripped their tickets in half and returned the stubs.
   (2) The girl's uncle gripped her hand tightly so the passing crowd wouldn't separate them.
   (3) They entered the circus.
   (4) The girl tugged her uncle's sleeve to try to get him to walk faster.
   (5) Helen wondered why her uncle was walking so slowly.

7. Which of the following is most likely to happen after this passage?
   (1) The circus isn't as good as Helen hoped.
   (2) Helen's uncle finds the circus magical.
   (3) Helen becomes impatient with her uncle.
   (4) Helen has a wonderful time at the circus.
   (5) Helen gets lost in the crowd.

8. What can you infer about the uncle?
   (1) He wishes his niece would slow down.
   (2) He cares a lot about his niece.
   (3) He is unreasonable about being so slow.
   (4) He is too generous with his niece.
   (5) He is forceful but loving toward his niece.

9. Which of the following phrases best describes Helen?
   (1) impatient and ill-behaved
   (2) sheltered and unrealistic
   (3) understanding and mature
   (4) cheerful and excited
   (5) chatty and hopeful

10. Which of the following phrases best describes the tone of this passage?
   (1) conversational and informative
   (2) peaceful and thoughtful
   (3) suspenseful and lively
   (4) serious and formal
   (5) warm and upbeat

WHAT TYPE OF FRUIT IS THIS WOMAN ENJOYING?

Beside the highway
at the motel door it roots
the last survivor of a pioneer orchard
miraculously still bearing.

5   A thud another apple falls I stoop and O
that scent, gnarled, ciderish with sun in it
that woody pulp for teeth and tongue to bite and curl around
that spurting juice earth-sweet!

In fifty seconds, fifty swimmers sweep and shake me—
10   I am alive! can stand up still
hoarding this apple in my hand.

"Eve"
By Dorothy Livesay

11. What does the detail "ciderish with sun in it" describe?
    (1) the apple tree
    (2) the door of the motel
    (3) the scent of the apple
    (4) the taste of the apple
    (5) the appearance of the apple

12. Which of the following best describes the effect of the rhythm in the last stanza?
    (1) It imitates short bursts of flavor.
    (2) It glides gently back and forth.
    (3) It creates sadness over the last apple.
    (4) It feels tense as if something will happen soon.
    (5) It creates a peaceful feeling of a pretty day.

13. What is meant by "fifty swimmers sweep / and shake me" (line 9)?
    (1) Swimmers walk by and splash her.
    (2) There are fifty more apples on the ground.
    (3) The apple's juice squirts into her mouth.
    (4) Fifty people before her ate apples here.
    (5) There are fifty other visitors at the motel.

14. Which of the following words best describes the mood of the poem?
    (1) curious
    (2) delighted
    (3) surprised
    (4) disinterested
    (5) thoughtful

15. Which of the following best states the theme of the poem?
    (1) Great pleasures can be found in unlikely places.
    (2) Nature always survives tough circumstances.
    (3) Enjoying nature will keep you from feeling lonely.
    (4) Apples are precious and should be enjoyed and hoarded.
    (5) The pleasure of fruit is worth trying to describe.

Questions 16 through 20 are based on the selection from a play below.

WHY IS LOMOV DRESSED SO FORMALLY?

CHUBUKOV (*Rising*): Well, look who's here! Ivan Vassilevitch! (*Shakes his hand warmly*) What a surprise, old man! How are you?

5   LOMOV: Oh, not too bad. And you?

CHUBUKOV: Oh, we manage, we manage. Do sit down, please. You know, you've been neglecting your neighbours, my dear fellow. It's
10   been ages. Say, why the formal dress? Tails, gloves, and so forth. Where's the funeral, my boy? Where are you headed?

LOMOV: Oh, nowhere. I mean, here;
15   just to see you, my dear Stepan Stepanovitch.

CHUBUKOV: Then why the full dress, old boy? It's not New Year's, and so forth.

20   LOMOV: Well, you see, it's like this. I have come here, my dear Stepan Stepanovitch, to bother you with a request. More than once, or twice, or more than that, it has been my
25   privilege to apply to you for assistance in things, and you've always, well, responded. I mean, well, you have. Yes. Excuse me, I'm getting all mixed up. May I have a
30   glass of water, my dear Stepan Stepanovitch? (*Drinks*)

CHUBUKOV (*Aside*): Wants to borrow some money. Not a chance! (*Aloud*) What can I do for you
35   my dear friend?

LOMOV: Well, you see, my dear Stepanitch . . . Excuse me, I mean Stepan my Dearovitch . . . No, I mean, I get all confused,
40   as you can see. To make a long story short, you're the only one who can help me. Of course, I don't deserve it, and there's no reason why I should expect you
45   to, and all that.

CHUBUKOV: Stop beating around the bush! Out with it!

LOMOV: In just a minute. I mean, now, right now. The truth is, I have
50   come to ask the hand . . . I mean, your daughter, Natalya, Stepanovna, I, I want to marry her!

CHUBUKOV (*Overjoyed*): Great heavens! Ivan Vassilevitch!

From *A Marriage Proposal*
By Anton Chekhov

16. Why does Chubukov say, "Then why the full dress, old boy? It's not New Year's, and so forth" (lines 17–19)?
    (1) Chubukov is angry at Lomov for dressing so fancily.
    (2) Chubukov doesn't understand why Lomov is all dressed up.
    (3) Chubukov believes there's a funeral.
    (4) Chubukov worries he's forgotten an important event.
    (5) Chubukov takes offense at the formality.

17. What is suggested by Chubukov saying, "Wants to borrow some money. Not a chance!"?
    (1) Chubukov will probably turn down Lomov's request.
    (2) Chubukov has always had bad feelings toward Lomov.
    (3) Chubukov pretends not to know why Lomov is visiting.
    (4) Chubukov is now poor and doesn't have any more money.
    (5) Chubukov wants Lomov to stand on his own without help.

18. Which of the following statements would Lomov most likely agree with?
    (1) Things could be worse.
    (2) People rarely get ahead in life.
    (3) First impressions are important.
    (4) It's always darkest before the dawn.
    (5) The early bird catches the worm.

19. Which of the following statements best describes Lomov's conflict?
    (1) He must be nice, but he dislikes Chubukov.
    (2) He is afraid that Chubukov won't think he is good enough for Natalya.
    (3) He worries that his nerves may cost Chubukov's approval.
    (4) He owes money but doesn't want to ask Chubukov for it.
    (5) He is angry with himself for not visiting Chubukov sooner.

20. Later, Lomov says, "I'm happy. Natalya . . . (*Kisses her hand*) My foot's gone to sleep." Based on this line and the passage, what can you assume about the tone of this play?

    It is
    (1) humorous
    (2) tragic
    (3) passionate
    (4) romantic
    (5) sarcastic

Reading Pretest Answers and Explanations

1. **(5) This was the first time Greene experienced not being good enough.** (Comprehension) The final sentence in the passage is, "For the first time in my life, I had been told officially that I wasn't good enough." This realization is what made the boy cry.

2. **(5) was surprised and unprepared** (Comprehension) The author mentions that he didn't know the cut was coming that day, and he kept looking at the list, hoping to find his name there.

3. **(3) You're a worthwhile person, no matter what happens.** (Application) The author was upset about not making the team. As an adult, he put this into perspective. Just because he was cut from the team, this didn't make him a bad person. It makes sense that he would share this lesson with his child if he or she were in a similar situation.

4. **(4) It sets up an emotionally important story.** (Analysis) The use of the phrase "remember vividly" lets the reader know that the author is writing about a critical experience. The mention of crying indicates that the story is emotional.

5. **(1) sad but heartwarming stories** (Synthesis) Both pieces by this writer have sad stories: the unwed mother not completing school and the boy shocked at not making the team. But these stories are also heartwarming; the woman completes her education, and the boy grows up to understand what happened during that vulnerable time.

6. **(5) Helen wondered why her uncle was walking so slowly.** (Comprehension) Helen's wondering why her uncle is going so slowly happens at the beginning of the second paragraph, before all the other events mentioned.

7. **(4) Helen has a wonderful time at the circus.** (Application) Helen has been looking forward to the circus for weeks and is amazed by every little thing that occurs. She will most likely have a great time at the circus. There is no evidence in the passage to support the other options.

8. **(2) He cares a lot about his niece.** (Analysis) He takes her to the circus and is very patient with and protective of her. (He makes sure they don't get separated.)

9. **(4) cheerful and excited** (Analysis) Helen's anticipation of the circus "tinted her days with an unreal glow." Her hand is described as "eager."

10. **(5) warm and upbeat** (Synthesis) Affection is expressed between Helen and her uncle, and they both remain pleased despite Helen's trying to prod her uncle to move more quickly.

11. **(3) the scent of the apple** (Comprehension) These words follow the phrase "O / that scent."

12. **(1) It imitates short bursts of flavor.** (Analysis) The lines are very short and almost jolting, like the bursts of flavor in her mouth.

13. **(3) The apple's juice squirts into her mouth.** (Analysis) The swimmers are most likely drops of juice from the apple that burst in her mouth and wake up her being. "I am alive!" she states after the swimmers "shake her."

14. **(2) delighted** (Synthesis) In the second stanza, the person describes the joy of the apple, "ciderish / with sun in it" and "that spurting juice / earth-sweet!"

15. **(1) Great pleasures can be found in unlikely places.** (Synthesis) The apple tree, left over from a former orchard, is now barely alive next to the highway motel—an unlikely place for an apple tree. But the apple provides significant pleasure to the speaker in the poem.

16. **(2) Chubukov doesn't understand why Lomov is all dressed up.** (Comprehension) Chubukov truly doesn't understand why Lomov is dressed up. He is unaware that Lomov wants his daughter's hand in marriage.

17. **(1) Chubukov will probably turn down Lomov's request.** (Comprehension) At this point in the play, the reader most likely thinks that Chubukov will say no to Lomov's request, since Chubukov already plans to say no to him if he asks for money.

18. **(3) First impressions are important.** (Application) Because Lomov has taken the trouble to dress up in order to ask for Natalya's hand in marriage, he realizes that impressions are important, even if this isn't a first impression since he already knows Chubukov.

19. **(2) He is afraid that Chubukov won't think he is good enough for Natalya.** (Analysis) Lomov's sole purpose in this excerpt is to gain Chubukov's approval for marrying Natalya. The conflict comes from the uncertainty about whether he will get this approval.

20. **(1) humorous** (Synthesis) The mention of his foot going to sleep is farcical, comical. It is out of place after kissing Natalya's hand. Also humorous is the nervous mixing up of Chubukov's name ("Dearovitch," for example).

Pretest Evaluation Chart

Follow these steps for the most effective use of this chart.

- Check your answers against the answers and explanations on page 12.
- Use the following chart to circle the questions you answered correctly.
- Total your correct answers in each row (across) for types of reading materials and each column (down) for thinking skills.

You can use the results to determine which types of reading and skills you need to focus on.

- The column on the left of the table indicates the KET Pre-GED video program and its corresponding lesson in this workbook.
- The column headings—*Comprehension, Application, Analysis,* and *Synthesis*—refer to the type of thinking skills needed to answer the questions.

SUBJECT AREAS AND THINKING SKILLS

Program	Comprehension	Application	Analysis	Synthesis	Total for Reading Subjects
7 Nonfiction (pp. 14–33)	1, 2	3	4	5	____/5
8 Fiction (pp. 34–53)	6	7	8, 9	10	____/5
9 Poetry (pp. 54–73)	11		12, 13	14, 15	____/5
10 Drama (pp. 74–93)	16, 17	18	19	20	____/5
Total for Skills	____/6	____/3	____/6	____/5	

Nonfiction

LESSON GOALS

READING SKILLS

- Understand what you read
- See relationships among ideas
- Analyze what you read

GED TEST-TAKING SKILLS

- Answering GED questions

READING & WRITING CONNECTION

- Writing a nonfiction story

GED REVIEW

1. Think About the Topic

About one-fourth of the questions on the GED Reading Test are about nonfiction passages. As you will see in the program, nonfiction is about real people and situations. On the test, you will read two nonfiction passages and answer multiple-choice questions about them.

In this program you will be introduced to nonfiction by a woman with her own day-care business, a film critic who uses both facts and opinions, and a writer who shares the details of his challenging childhood.

2. Prepare to Watch the Video

This program will give you an overview of several types of nonfiction: instruction manuals, movie reviews, and autobiographies. Think of the people you will meet in the video—a day-care owner, a film critic, and a writer. What type of nonfiction reading do you think these people might do? List some possibilities below.

Day-Care Owner

_____

Film Critic

_____

Writer

_____

You may have said *The film critic may read reviews or biographies to get information on the people in the film.*

3. Preview the Questions

Read the questions under *Think About the Program*, and keep them in mind as you watch the program. You will review them after you watch.

4. Study the Vocabulary

Review the terms to the right. Understanding the meaning of key nonfiction vocabulary will help you understand the video and the rest of this lesson.

WATCH THE PROGRAM

As you watch the program, pay special attention to the host who introduces or summarizes major nonfiction ideas that you need to learn about. The host will also give you important information about the GED Reading Test.

AFTER YOU WATCH

1. Think About the Program

Which would you prefer to write, fiction or nonfiction? Why?

How do you tell the difference between fact and opinion in nonfiction writing?

How should you decide when to read a whole document carefully or when you should skim for important details?

In what types of nonfiction writing does the writer show his or her viewpoint or bias?

In what kind of nonfiction writing does the writer mainly stick to the facts?

2. Make the Connection

Try writing a nonfiction piece. Pick an issue in your neighborhood and write a magazine article, or write a short story about something interesting that happened to you recently.

bias—the tendency to lean toward one particular point of view

cause—event that leads to another event

compare—describe what is the same about two people, places, or things

conclusion—something you reason out based on your understanding

contrast—describe what is different between two people, places, or things

effect—result of a cause

fact—information that can be proved

inference—something you assume without being told

main idea—point the writer is trying to get across

opinion—statement of feelings and beliefs

supporting detail—fact or example that backs up the writer's point

tone—the writer's attitude toward a subject

"I don't like made-up stories because they're not as interesting. True stories are more fun because they hit close to home."

Understanding What You Read

Main Ideas

As the host stated in the video, the **main idea** is the point the writer wants to make. Sometimes the main idea is stated directly, as in the example below. Often, the main idea is the paragraph's first sentence.

EXAMPLE

Biographies make history fun to learn. Most biographies contain facts about interesting personalities. They also follow that person's life all the way through. As I get familiar with the person, I get more and more interested in finding out what happened to him or her.

What is the main point the writer is trying to make about biographies?

_____

The first sentence is a possible answer: *Biographies make history fun to learn.*

Sometimes the main idea is not directly stated. When this happens, you can figure out what the main idea is from details in the passage.

Supporting Details

Supporting details help create the main idea. So if you want to get across the main idea that you enjoy life, you could write something like this:

EXAMPLE

I usually laugh at things that annoy most people. I sleep like a baby, and I get along with my family.

Reread the biography example at the top of this page. What are two details that the writer gives to explain why biographies make history fun for her to learn?

1. _____

2. _____

You may have written something like *facts about interesting personalities* or *learning a lot about one person's life*. Those details explain why biographies make history fun to learn.

See page 115 for a *Main Idea and Details Cluster Diagram*.

READING SKILLS

A. Read the nonfiction passage below. This passage is about the writer's mother.

Her father, Robert Lee, abandoned the family just before she was born, and Mama lost her mother in childbirth when she was only four. She was left to grow up without affection or closeness or indulgence. Yet she wasn't thrown into an orphanage or adopted or shuttled around to foster families. She lived at first with
5 her grandmother, then in the teeming household of her aunt and uncle. Her kinfolks took her in, out of obligation. But they gave her little love. "You're lucky to have a roof over your head," they said as they put her to work. She says she felt like a lost kitten, crouching beneath the passing shadow of a hawk.

For me, the image that most illuminates her childhood is the Christmas orange.
10 One Christmas, in the houseful of kinfolks she was raised with at Clear Springs, the older cousins got dolls, but all she got was an orange.

She remembers how, as the smallest child in the household, she was made to work in the garden, the fields, the tobacco patch. "I was just an extra mouth to feed," Mama says bitterly.

From *Clear Springs: A Memoir*
By Bobbie Ann Mason

B. Choose the correct answer to the question below.

1. Which of the following is the main point Bobbie Ann Mason wants to make with this passage?
   a. Her mother got only an orange for Christmas.
   b. Her mother grew up "without affection or closeness or indulgence."
   c. Her mother was not given up for adoption or foster care.
   d. Her mother's father abandoned his wife and children.

C. Choose the detail that best supports each of these main ideas.

2. For me, the image that most illuminates her childhood is the Christmas orange.
   a. "but all she got was an orange"
   b. "houseful of kinfolks"

3. She was left to grow up without affection or closeness or indulgence.
   a. "She lived at first with her grandmother, then in the teeming household of her aunt and uncle."
   b. "But they gave her little love."

Answers and explanations start on page 106.

Making Inferences

An **inference** is something you conclude without being told directly. For example, if you read that two people are married, you might infer that they live together.

EXAMPLE

Some horse trainers use signals to communicate with horses. For example, trainers will turn their backs and walk away when they want a horse to follow. Trainers will raise their hands, palms outward and move them back and forth to send a horse away. The horse's body language shows if the animal is trying to cooperate. Good signs are licking the lips or nodding the head.

1. Based on the paragraph, what do you infer is the meaning of the term *body language?*

_____

You may have said something like *Body language consists of motions that show feelings.*

Drawing Conclusions

When you draw a **conclusion,** you figure out information based on inferences. For example, if you infer that a married couple lives together, you might conclude that they know each other's habits.

EXAMPLE

A monkey grins to show that it wants to please you. It may peel back its lips to say, "Let's play." If the monkey lies down on its back, it's saying that you are in charge. If it pounds its fists, it may be saying you are not in charge.

2. Suppose you infer that humans use body language in the same way animals do. What can you conclude about someone who grins at a police officer who has pulled him over for speeding?

_____

A possible answer is: *He is trying to show he wants to please the officer to avoid getting a ticket.*

3. How did you draw this conclusion?

_____

Possible answer: *A human shows willingness to please with a grin just as a monkey does.*

A. Read the nonfiction passage below.

It is a quiet town, where much of the day you could stand in the middle of Main Street and not be in anyone's way—not forever, but for as long as a person would want to stand in the middle of a street...

5 Most men wear their belts low here, there being so many outstanding bellies, some big enough to have names of their own and be formally introduced. Those men don't suck them in or hide them in loose shirts; they let them hang free, they pat them, they stroke them as they stand around and talk. How could a man be so vain as to ignore this old friend who's been with him at the great moments of his life?

The buildings are quite proud in their false fronts, trying to be everything that
10 two stories can be and a little bit more... A child might have cut them off a cornflakes box and fastened them with two tabs, A and B, and added the ladies leaving the Chatterbox Cafe from their tuna sandwich lunch.

From *Lake Wobegon Days*
By Garrison Keillor

B. Read the following inferences based on this passage. Give the reason why each inference was made.

> **Example:** This passage is meant to be funny.
> **Reason:** Garrison Keillor says surprising things, such as the bellies having their own names.

1. Garrison Keillor, the author, likes this town.
   Reason: _____
2. The citizens want their town to look impressive.
   Reason: _____
3. Residents in the town are comfortable in public.
   Reason: _____
4. People in the town are not concerned about physical appearances.
   Reason: _____

C. Make a check mark next to the inference on which the conclusion is based.

5. There isn't much traffic in the town.

   ❏ **a.** You could stand in the middle of the street and not be in the way.

   ❏ **b.** Men have their own social groups.

Answers and explanations start on page 106.

"I have no position on the issue before us, To stay in L.A. To go. What does it matter? I've been a red-hot ball, bouncing around from here to there. Anyone can bounce me."

Seeing Relationships Among Ideas

Compare

In the video, the writer compares himself to a red-hot ball. To **compare** is to describe what is the same about two people, places, or things. How is a raven like a robin? *Both are birds.* Read the example below, and notice the comparison that the pet groomer makes.

> **EXAMPLE**
>
> As a pet groomer, I see how owners' personalities seem to match those of their pets. A typical dog owner wants unquestioning loyalty and love from a pet and is willing to give the dog the same loyalty and care. They'd be very uneasy with the independent, self-absorbed cat. A cat owner, however, likes personal freedom as the cat does. He or she relates to an animal that can take care of itself and doesn't depend on a human for company.

1. How is the dog owner like the dog?

   _____

A possible answer is: *Both want a lot of loyalty and closeness from the other.*

2. How is the cat owner like the cat?

   _____

A possible answer is: *Both of them like to have their personal freedom.*

Contrast

To **contrast** is to identify differences between two things, people, or places. Read the pet owner example again, and answer the question below.

3. What does the pet groomer say is a difference between dog owners and cat owners?

   _____

You may have written something like *Dog owners want more loyalty than cat owners do.* Or you could have said, *Cat owners want more independence than dog owners do.*

See the *Compare and Contrast Venn Diagram* on page 116.

A. Read the nonfiction article below.

The construction of Jefferson College's second library is finally complete. The new Alumni Memorial Library, which is located on the other end of campus from the current Davidson Library, is scheduled to open this Monday.

The first two floors of the Memorial Library will remind visitors of the Davidson.
5 Although the architecture is different, the content and layout of the floors are very much the same. The Memorial Library, like the Davidson, will offer students plenty of room for quiet study and a large collection of reference materials, periodicals, and books.

The third floor of the Memorial Library is where you will find the difference.
10 It contains two large computer labs that will allow students access to the card catalogs of other local libraries. The computers also contain a large database of newspapers and magazines. The online collection of these materials at the Memorial is much greater than the hard-copy collection the Davidson can maintain. The computers will be an invaluable resource to students.

15 The library will be open 6 days a week from 7:00 A.M. to 10:00 P.M. The library is open to students, and unlike the Davidson, it will also be open to graduates of the university who show an alumni card.

B. Write *Compare* (for similarity) or *Contrast* (for differences) next to each statement.

_____ 1. The content and layout of the floors are very much the same.

_____ 2. The Memorial Library, like the Davidson, will offer students plenty of room for quiet study.

_____ 3. The library is open to students, and unlike the Davidson, it will also be open to graduates of the university who show an alumni card.

C. List two similarities and two differences related the libraries discussed above.

4. Similarities

_____   _____

5. Differences

_____   _____

Answers and explanations start on page 106.

Cause and Effect

A **cause** is an event that leads to another event. An **effect** is the result of the cause. A cause can have more than one effect, and an effect can have more than one cause. For example, if you woke up late, one effect might be that you miss the bus. Another effect might be that you had to walk to work. There may have also been more than one thing that caused you to wake up late. For example, one cause may be that you were up late the night before, and another may be that your alarm was broken.

Try to identify the different cause-and-effect relationships present in the passage below.

EXAMPLE

When a substance is heated, its molecules move faster, and that causes it to expand. When matter is cooled, molecules move slower, and the substance contracts, gets smaller. When a solid is heated enough so that its molecules vibrate fast enough to break the bond between them, the solid melts. When a solid melts, it becomes a liquid. When the liquid is heated further, the molecules move even faster and more energetically. Eventually, they move enough to free them from the liquid altogether. That's when the liquid is said to boil.

Adapted from *Dictionary of Scientific Literacy*
By Richard P. Brennan

1. What causes molecules to move faster inside a substance?

_____

You could have said *heat*.

2. What is the effect of cooling on a substance?

_____

You may have said something like *The substance contracts, gets smaller.*

3. What is the effect of the bond between molecules breaking apart in a solid?

_____

You probably said, *The solid becomes a liquid.*

4. What causes molecules to get closer together?

_____

You probably said *cooling them.*

See page 117 for a *Cause-and-Effect Chain*.

A. Read the nonfiction passage below.

I woke up at 2:30 this morning after about five hours' sleep. The lights of the little artificial Christmas tree were sweet in the living room. I went to put on coffee. But when I realized how early it was, I decided against it. Instead, I made some oatmeal with fresh apple and cinnamon.

5 Then I pulled the blanket off our pet rabbit's cage and checked in with him. He seemed eager to get food and attention unexpectedly. But he made very little noise about it. I ate my oatmeal sitting in my cushy, old armchair and just enjoyed the peaceful feeling.

Then I went back to sleep until about 7:00. I was done with my errands and
10 responsibilities by about lunchtime. So I worked without pressure this afternoon. Now, it's almost 5:00 P.M., and I still feel good.

Ahhh. A day without the kids.

B. Match each of the causes in the left column with the correct effect in the right column.

_____ 1. decided not to put the coffee on   **a.** at 5 P.M., still feel good

_____ 2. pulled the blanket off the rabbit's cage   **b.** animal seemed eager to get food

_____ 3. done with errands by lunchtime   **c.** felt no pressure in the afternoon

_____ 4. a day without children   **d.** had oatmeal instead

C. Check all of the choices that are likely.

5. What are some possible effects of the writer's day off from her children?

❑ **a.** She will enjoy them more when they come back home.

❑ **b.** The children will have missed her.

❑ **c.** She will not feel pressured in the afternoons anymore.

❑ **d.** The writer will decide to get up at 2:30 every morning.

❑ **e.** The children will start eating oatmeal daily.

Answers and explanations start on page 106.

Analyzing What You Read

Fact

In the video, you learned that **facts** are pieces of information that can be proved. For example, by looking at a map, you could prove that *Somalia is a country in Africa.* You could check an almanac to prove that *the population of Essex, Massachusetts, is about six hundred seventy thousand.*

As you read the passage below, look for facts.

EXAMPLE

In 1997 my kids and I took a road trip to Asheville, North Carolina. We stayed in Travelodge motels in Chambersburg, Pennsylvania, and Roanoke, Virginia. We stayed with friends in Asheville and in Silver Springs, Maryland. The trip took eight adventure-filled days, and we had the best time.

The car radio didn't work, so we listened to tapes over and over. My son's favorite cut was "Get Up, Stand Up" by Bob Marley. My daughter's and mine were both from the same tape by a Canadian folksinger. Robin liked the angry song about women on welfare. I liked the sentimental one about men with the courage to cry. We all ended up learning each other's favorites, singing along, and poking fun at each other.

1. Write two statements that contain facts from the passage above.

_____

_____

You may have written something like, *Asheville is in North Carolina,* or *The family took their trip in 1997.*

Opinion

Opinions are statements that express feelings and beliefs. When you read nonfiction, it is important to distinguish a writer's opinion from the facts.

2. Write one example of an opinion from the passage.

_____

One answer is: *We had the best time.* This statement expresses the author's feelings about the trip.

A. Read the nonfiction passage below. This movie description is based on one that appears in a published movie guide.

The Quiet Man

Academy Awards: Best Picture and Best Cinematographer, 1952
Cast [Lead Actors]: John Wayne, Maureen O'Hara
Director: John Ford
Color

5 153 minutes

One of John Ford's greatest and most loved films is this comedy, love story, and love letter to Ford's Irish homeland. John Wayne plays a boxer who has come back to his birthplace, the small village of Innisfree. He loses his heart to the town bully's beautiful sister, who is played by Maureen O'Hara, never lovelier than

10 she is in this role. The couple's rivalry comes to an explosive, hilarious climax when O'Hara refuses to consider herself married until Wayne receives her dowry [property gift from bride to groom] from her brother. The secretive American finally unleashes his fists and earns his wife's love and respect. Ford's brother appears as an old man who refuses to die until he sees the men battle.

Paraphrase of a review from *American Movie Classics' Classic Movie Companion,* 1999
Edited by Robert Moses

B. Read each sentence and write the word that makes the sentence an opinion.

1. This is one of John Ford's greatest films. _____
2. John Wayne is perfect for this part. _____
3. Maureen O'Hara had gorgeous auburn hair. _____
4. Having a dowry is a ridiculous idea. _____
5. The climax of this film is hilarious. _____

C. Mark each statement about the film as *F* for fact or *O* for opinion.

6. _____ John Ford directed John Wayne in *The Quiet Man.*
7. _____ Ford's brother, Francis, does a funny scene.
8. _____ In the film, Maureen O'Hara plays the town bully's sister.
9. _____ Innisfree is a town in Ireland.
10. _____ Maureen O'Hara has never been lovelier than she was in this film.

Answers and explanations start on page 106.

Synthesizing Ideas

Tone is the overall feeling the writer wants you to get from the reading. The style of the writing will often determine whether the tone is sad, happy, suspenseful, or humorous.

Read the two paragraphs below. What type of feeling do they leave you with?

EXAMPLES

My family takes pictures instead of talking to each other when we get together. If we're not taking pictures, we're looking at old pictures and discussing them. We can't seem to face the real us.

My family takes pictures at every get-together. We also bring pictures from previous gatherings. We'll never forget the good times we've had.

1. What is the tone of the first paragraph?

_____

Possible answers are *sad, frustrated,* or *disgusted.*

2. What is the tone of the writer of the second paragraph?

_____

You may have said something like *happy* or *reflective.*

Bias is a preference for one point of view. Personal experiences and beliefs shape a person's bias. Think about the writer's bias in the following two statements.

EXAMPLES

First writer: His job should always be a man's first priority. He can't take care of his family if he doesn't do a proper job at work.

Second writer: His family should always be a man's top concern. He's not going to say to himself on his deathbed, "I wish I had worked harder at my job." He's going to want to have spent more time with his loved ones.

3. The first writer's bias is *(for, against)* making work the man's top priority.

You should have said *for.*

4. The second writer's bias is *(for, against)* making work the man's top priority.

You should have said *against.*

A. Read the nonfiction passage below.

Also in 1964, the Warren Commission released its report on the John F. Kennedy assassination. The commission concluded that Lee Harvey Oswald acted alone, and that settled that.

I am of course kidding. Within [seconds] of the release of the Warren
5 Commission report, a new American industry sprang up: the Paranoia Industry, which has grown over the decades to the point where it now employs three out of every ten Americans, and which has produced a [large] body of solid evidence proving beyond a shadow of a doubt that Kennedy was in fact killed by a [huge] conspiracy whose members include ... the FBI, the CIA, the military, big business,
10 the Mafia, the Communists, the media, the Trilateral Commission, ... as well as both Chad *and* Jeremy [1960s musical duo].

From *Dave Barry Turns 50*
By Dave Barry

B. Write your answers to the questions below in the space provided.

1. What is the tone of the passage above? _____

2. What word in the first sentence of the second paragraph shows the writer's tone?

   _____

3. Write a word or phrase that helps create the tone in the piece. Explain.

   _____

   _____

C. Write *For* or *Against* to describe the bias shown in the statement below. Then write the reason for your answer.

Example: Doctors think they know everything. I wouldn't trust one not to burn a pancake.

For or Against? ____Against____ Reason: ____The person doesn't trust doctors.____

4. Football is too dangerous a sport for young children to play. Several kids have already been seriously injured this year.

   For or Against? _____ Reason: _____

Answers and explanations start on page 107.

Answering GED Questions

On the GED Reading Test, you will read a passage and then answer a series of multiple-choice questions about the selection. Each question gives five possible answers, and you will choose the one that makes the most sense.

EXAMPLE

Next to writing, cab driving was my favorite job ever. There was so much freedom in it. You work without direct supervision. You work alone, yet you meet new people all the time. You get to travel around, and in between trips, you can read or gossip with the other drivers. Like a writer, you collect great stories about people's lives as they pass through your cab. In fact, taxi driving is the perfect second job for a writer.

Which of the following is a similarity between cab drivers and writers?
(1) Both collect stories.
(2) Both are interested in people.
(3) Neither earns high income.
(4) Cabbies work alone.
(5) Cabbies have to be good at conversation.

The correct answer is **(1) Both collect stories.** This answer is correct because it is the only one that describes both writers and cabbies.

What did the question ask? It asked about the similarity between cabbies and writers. Think through all the choices. One may seem right, but you need to check all of them.

- **Eliminate answers that don't relate to the question.** Choices (4) and (5) are not about similarities.

- **Eliminate answers that may relate to the topic but are not discussed in the passage.** Choice (3) is not discussed in the passage.

- **Make a decision between two appealing choices.** Choices (1) and (2) seem like similarities at first. When you stop and think, though, you realize writers might use buildings or animals or anything else as their subjects rather than people. Only (1) is a similarity.

TEST-TAKING HINTS
- Eliminate answers that don't relate to the question.
- Eliminate answers that are not discussed in the passage.
- Make a decision between two appealing choices.

Sample GED Question

We have a family tree with many roots. Robin was adopted from South America, Kai, from Central America. I am second-generation Irish from Boston, and Bob is one-quarter Cherokee from Kentucky. Each of the kids has two sets of roots, ours and their birth families' in Latin America. Even though none of us look alike,

5 we are a family, and I'm closer to them than to anyone else. Still, it would make an odd-looking tree. Maybe we should call it a family vine.

Which statement is the main idea of the paragraph?

(1) Members of the family don't look like each other.

(2) The parents don't keep the adoptions secret.

(3) Adoptive families are as close as biological families.

(4) Some adopted children come from Latin America.

(5) Adoption crosses country borders.

You can eliminate choices (1) and (4) because they are not main ideas. You can eliminate (2) because it doesn't relate directly to the passage. Both (5) and (3) are good choices, but **(3) Adoptive families are as close as biological families** is a better main idea because the writer talks about the closeness of her family.

GED TEST-TAKING SKILL PRACTICE

ANSWERING GED QUESTIONS

Questions 1 and 2 are based on the passage below.

The best movie I've seen this year is *I Am Sam,* the story of a mentally retarded father who doesn't want to lose custody of his daughter. The two have a genuine parent-child relationship even though she is about to pass by him in book learning.

5 The lead role is played beautifully by Sean Penn, who usually plays a loner or tough guy. His ability to play a different type of role is revealed in *I Am Sam.*

Despite the sensitive subject matter and an emotionally moving soundtrack, *I Am Sam* is far from depressing; it is exhilarating and optimistic.

1. Which of the following is the movie about?

(1) Sean Penn

(2) fatherhood

(3) intelligent children

(4) mental retardation

(5) acting

2. What is the main idea of this review?

(1) Sean Penn is a great actor.

(2) Children are smarter than their parents.

(3) *I Am Sam* is a good movie worth seeing.

(4) The movie's soundtrack is very moving.

(5) Not everyone is capable of being a father.

Answers and explanations start on page 107.

Writing a Nonfiction Story

You can use what you have learned in this program about reading nonfiction to help you write your own nonfiction story about a personal experience you've had recently. You can use a 5 *W*s chart like the one below to organize your ideas for writing.

WRITING TOPIC

What is one personal experience that led to your decision to study for the GED?

Who?	Marina
What?	Became manager
When?	In January
Where?	At beauty salon where I work
Why?	She had passed her GED.

Here is a sample nonfiction story based on the chart above.

> When the position of manager became available at the beauty salon where I work, I thought for sure that I would get the promotion. Instead the promotion went to Marina. I was so angry. I couldn't believe it; I had a lot more experience than she had. She got the promotion in January after only six months on the job! I had been there for almost a year! The owner told me that she wanted to promote me, but she couldn't because I didn't have my high-school diploma. Marina saw how angry I was, and she did me a big favor. She told me how she had passed her GED and encouraged me to get mine as well. It was the best advice that I ever got.

STORY-WRITING HINTS
- Use events that create strong feelings in you.
- Use words to show time order, like *when* and *after*.
- Read aloud and try to hear any errors or confusing parts in your story.

See the 5 Ws Chart on page 118.

A. Reread the topic on page 30. Fill in the chart with your own personal information.

Who?	
What?	
When?	
Where?	
Why?	

B. On another piece of paper, write one or two paragraphs based on the information that you filled in on the chart above.

C. Self-Check Questions

Did the chart help you to write the about the paragraphs?

_____

_____

If it helped, how did it help you?

_____

_____

Did you need all five *W*s? Why or why not? _____

_____

_____

Which *W*s were the most helpful to you? Why?

_____

_____

Answers and explanations start on page 107.

GED Review: Nonfiction

Choose the <u>one best answer</u> to the questions below.

Questions 1 through 5 refer to the following article.

HOW DID THE FARMERS SOLVE THEIR PROBLEM?

A neighborhood in Boise, Idaho, had five new families in it. They had had their own farms outside the city. But then they were forced to sell out to
5 a big farm corporation. They were all pretty unhappy until one of them came up with a clever idea.

A one-acre lot in the Boise neighborhood was for sale. One of the
10 farmers suggested that the five families buy the land together and run it as a farm cooperative.

They could sell their produce in the city at lower prices than the grocery
15 stores could offer. They could work the land in equal shifts and share the profits equally.

One of the other farmers even had a plan for the winter months. They
20 could raise turkeys, pumpkins, and evergreen trees for sale in October, November, and December.

All the farmers were very happy that they didn't have to give up the work
25 they loved. Boise residents enjoyed having a source of fresh, inexpensive produce right in the city.

1. Why did the farmers move to the city?
   (1) They wanted closer neighbors.
   (2) They sold to a big farm corporation.
   (3) They were tired of farming.
   (4) The rural land was too crowded.
   (5) They wanted to farm fewer crops.

2. Which of the following is an opinion related to the passage?
   (1) The farmers had to sell to a big farm corporation.
   (2) A one-acre lot was for sale in Boise.
   (3) The families worked together on a cooperative.
   (4) Grocery store prices are too high.
   (5) The farmers fought constantly.

3. What conclusion can you draw about the farmer who had the idea to buy the land?
   (1) He is imaginative.
   (2) He is greedy.
   (3) He likes his neighbors.
   (4) He likes to be with his family.
   (5) He enjoys eating produce.

4. Which would be the best title for the passage?
   (1) Farming in the City
   (2) Farmers Give Up
   (3) Eat Your Spinach
   (4) Escape to the Country
   (5) How to Grow Your Own Food

5. Which statement contrasts the Boise grocery stores with the farmers?
   (1) The stores sell produce.
   (2) The farmers charge lower prices than the stores.
   (3) The stores share profits.
   (4) They both sell fresh produce.
   (5) They both sell a wide variety of produce.

Questions 6 through 10 refer to the following article.

HOW DOES THE FAMILY DEAL WITH POVERTY?

There was no escaping their poverty, however. They lived now in the Bronx, in a one-bedroom apartment in a redbrick building on Tremont Avenue,
5   next to an Italian beer garden where the old men played bocce on summer evenings. Because of the Depression, Morrie's father found even less work in the fur business. Sometimes when
10 the family sat at the dinner table, all Eva could put out was bread.

"What else is there?" David would ask.

"Nothing else," she would answer.

15 When she tucked Morrie and David into bed, she would sing to them in Yiddish. Even the songs were sad and poor. There was one about a girl trying to sell her cigarettes:

20 *Please buy my cigarettes.*
They are dry, not wet by rain.
Take pity on me, take pity on me.

Still, despite their circumstances, Morrie was taught to love and to care.
25 And to learn. Eva would accept nothing less than excellence in school, because she saw education as the only antidote to their poverty. She herself went to night school to improve her English.
30 Morrie's love for education was hatched in her arms.

From *Tuesdays with Morrie*
By Mitch Albom

6. Which of the following statements is a fact?
   (1) The family lived in Manhattan.
   (2) The family lived on Tremont Avenue.
   (3) Eva would sing to the boys in English.
   (4) Eva didn't think school was important.
   (5) Morrie was sent to night school.

7. What is the tone of this passage?
   (1) positive
   (2) sad
   (3) angry
   (4) amused
   (5) disgusted

8. What was the cause behind Morrie's father struggling to find work?
   (1) not enough experience
   (2) not enough skill
   (3) not enough fur
   (4) the Depression
   (5) the First World War

9. What can you conclude about Eva?
   (1) She didn't like her life.
   (2) She was cold and unfeeling.
   (3) She was a wonderful singer.
   (4) She was proud and strong.
   (5) She sold cigarettes for a living.

10. What was the effect of Eva's attitude about education on her son, Morrie?
    (1) He disliked school.
    (2) He grew to love education.
    (3) He disliked his mother.
    (4) He decided to study Yiddish.
    (5) He went to medical school.

Answers and explanations start on page 107.

Fiction

LESSON GOALS

READING SKILLS

- Set the stage
- Picture the characters
- Tell the story

GED TEST-TAKING SKILLS

- Answering special synthesis questions

READING & WRITING CONNECTION

- Journal writing about fiction

GED REVIEW

1. Think About the Topic

Three-quarters of the questions on the GED Reading Test are based on fiction, including prose, poetry, and drama. In this program, you will learn about prose fiction.

Fiction writing is about imaginary situations and people. It includes short stories and novels. On the test, you will read fiction passages and answer multiple-choice questions about them. You'll use reading skills such as identifying conflict.

This program will introduce you to a young female author from Haiti and two famous fiction writers, Flannery O'Connor and Edgar Allan Poe.

2. Prepare to Watch the Video

In the program, you will get an overview of several ways of writing fiction. One way is to write as though you are the main character, using "I." Edgar Allan Poe wrote his chilling story "The Tell-Tale Heart" this way. What is your favorite novel or story? Was it told from the point of view of the main character or someone else? What did you like most about the story?

Favorite Novel or Story:

_____

Setting and Main Character:

_____

You might have said something like: *My favorite novel is* The Adventures of Tom Sawyer. *The story is told from the first person point of view. I liked the characters the best.*

3. Preview the Questions

Read the questions under *Think About the Program* and keep them in mind as you watch the program. You will review them after you watch.

4. Study the Vocabulary

Review the terms to the right. Understanding the meaning of key fiction vocabulary will help you understand the video and the rest of this lesson.

WATCH THE PROGRAM

As you watch the program, pay special attention to the host who introduces or summarizes major fiction ideas that you need to learn about. The host will also give you important information about the GED Reading Test.

 AFTER YOU WATCH

1. Think About the Program

What are some of the elements you find in fiction?

What do you think George Ella Lyon, the writer, meant when she said that the tone of a piece is like the "emotional weather forecast?"

What are some of the different types of conflict that can exist in a story?

What are the different points of view from which a story can be told?

2. Make the Connection

If you wrote a fiction story, who would the characters be? What would the setting be? What would be the conflict? What would the mood of your story be?

character development—creation of the person in a story who says and does things

conflict—struggle; can be within a character, between characters, or between a character and an outside force

first-person narrative—story told from the perspective of a character; uses "I"

mood—story's atmosphere, created through dialogue, details of the setting, and style

point of view—perspective from which the author writes; for example, first person is told from the perspective of a character and uses "I"

setting—time and place in which story occurs

sequence of events—order in which the action of a story takes place

"And, as though he commanded, Sonny began to play. Something began to happen. And Creole let out the reins. The dry, low black man said something awful on the drums, Creole answered, and the drums talked back."

Setting the Stage

Setting

This quote from the video gives some clues about how it feels and sounds to be in a room with musicians. Details like this help create the setting. The **setting** is the time and place in which a story occurs. A good writer uses specific words to bring the reader into the setting. Read the short passage below. As you read the passage try to create a picture in your mind. Where is this place? What does it look like? sound like? smell like? What types of feelings and tastes are portrayed?

EXAMPLE

It was a spring afternoon in West Florida. Janie had spent most of the day under a blossoming pear tree in the back-yard. She had been spending every minute that she could steal from her chores under that tree for the last three days. That was to say, ever since the first tiny bloom had opened. It had called her to come and gaze on a mystery. From barren brown stems to glistening leaf-buds; from the leaf-buds to snowy virginity of bloom. It stirred her tremendously. How? Why? It was like a flute song forgotten in another existence and remembered again.

From *Their Eyes Were Watching God*
By Zora Neale Hurston

1. What word or words in the example help you to "see" Zora Neale Hurston's setting?

_____

A possible answer is *"back-yard"* or *"under that tree."* These phrases bring specific pictures to your mind.

2. What time of year is this? What time of the day?

_____

You could have said *"a spring afternoon."*

3. Which phrase in the paragraph makes you "hear" or "feel" Hurston's setting?

_____

You could have said *"barren brown stems."* You can imagine what barren brown stems would feel like when touched. You can hear *"a flute song."*

A. Read the fiction passage below. This passage is about a factory town in England. Picture the place, and think about how it looks and smells.

It was a town of red brick, or of brick that would have been red if the smoke and ashes had allowed it; but as matters stood it was a town of unnatural red, and black . . . It was a town of machinery and tall chimneys, out of which interminable serpents of smoke trailed themselves forever and ever, and never got uncoiled. It had a black canal in it, and a river that ran purple with ill-smelling dye, and vast piles of buildings full of windows where there was a rattling and a trembling all day long, and where the piston of the steam-engine worked monotonously up and down like the head of an elephant in a state of melancholy madness. It contained several large streets all very like one another, and many small streets still more like one another, inhabited by people equally like one another.

From *Hard Times*
By Charles Dickens

B. Circle the words or phrases from the paragraph that help you to picture the setting.

1. Which phrase helps you to "see" the ugliness of this town?
   a. serpents of smoke   **b.** ill-smelling dye

2. Which phrase gives you the sense of boredom or depression in this town?
   a. rattling and trembling   **b.** worked monotonously up and down

3. Which phrase helps you to feel the unhealthy nature of this town?
   a. river that ran purple   **b.** rattling and trembling

4. Which phrase helps you to "hear" what the town sounds like?
   a. serpents of smoke   **b.** rattling and trembling

C. The selection does not directly tell you when this situation took place. However, Dickens wrote during the early years of the Industrial Revolution, when manufacturing was first being done by machines. Use this information to help you answer the question below.

5. Write one phrase that suggests that the setting of the passage is during the Industrial Revolution.

_____

_____

Answers and explanations start on page 108.

Mood

Mood is the atmosphere of the story. Mood is created by details of the setting. Some words you could use to describe the mood of a story are *gloomy, peaceful, joyful,* and *scary.*

EXAMPLE

That night she had a new consciousness of the country, felt almost a new relation to it. Even her talk with the boys had not taken away the feeling that had overwhelmed her when she drove back to the Divide that afternoon. She had never known before how much the country meant to her. The chirping of the insects down in the long grass had been like the sweetest music. She had felt as if her heart were hiding down there, somewhere, with the quail and the plover [a shore bird] and all the little wild things that crooned or buzzed in the sun. Under the long shaggy ridges, she felt the future stirring.

From *O Pioneers!*
By Willa Cather

1. What word would you use to describe the mood of this passage?

_____

You may have written something like *hopeful* or *positive.*

2. What phrases support the idea that the mood of this passage is hopeful?

_____

_____

Possible responses are *"new consciousness of the country"* and *"felt the future stirring."*

3. What sounds contribute to the positive mood of the passage?

_____

_____

Two possible responses are *"the chirping of the insects down in the long grass had been like the sweetest music"* or *"little wild things that crooned or buzzed in the sun."*

4. What mood is created by the details about the setting in the Hurston passage on page 36?

_____

One possible response is that the mood is *peaceful.*

A. Read the fiction passage below.

The path took us along to the side of the greenhouse and the butler opened a door for me and stood aside. It opened into a sort of vestibule that was about as warm as a slow oven. He came in after me, shut the outer door, opened an inner door and we went through that. Then it was really hot. The air was thick, wet,

5 steamy, and larded with the cloying smell of tropical orchids in bloom. The glass walls and roof were heavily misted and big drops of moisture splashed down on the plants. The light had an unreal greenish color, like light filtered through an aquarium tank. The plants filled the place, a forest of them, with nasty meaty leaves and stalks like the newly washed fingers of dead men.

From *The Big Sleep*
By Raymond Chandler

B. Write an X next to the correct answer.

Example:

What is the mood of the following piece?
A gentle breeze blew over the docks, carrying with it the smell of the sea. Small waves broke gently onto the shore as a flock of seagulls floated lazily in the sky.

   _X_ **a.** calm   _____ **b.** upset

1. What is the mood of the Chandler passage above?
   _____ **a.** comfortable   _____ **b.** mysterious

2. Which of the following phrases helps to create that mood?
   _____ **a.** The path took us along to the side of the greenhouse
   _____ **b.** The light had an unreal greenish color

C. Write the answer on the line.

Charlie took Joan by the hand and turned toward the water. She looked up at his strong, forward-seeking chin. The sun was rising behind their favorite bird-watching island, and she wondered if the snowy owl was waking up. With a sigh, Joan leaned happily against Charlie and closed her eyes.

3. What is one detail about the place that creates the peaceful mood of the passage above?

_____

Answers and explanations start on page 108.

"Remember that we're going to be like mountains, and mountains don't cry."

Picturing the Characters

Character Development

The quote above is from one of the characters in the video. They are the words from an aunt to her niece, who is going on a trip. The characters are the people in the story who say and do things. **Character development** is when the writer makes the character say and do things to help show their personality. In other words, the writer uses dialogue and action to bring the character to life.

Read the passage below, and see how the writer makes the character of Zeke comes to life.

EXAMPLE

Zeke grew up hanging around his uncle's gas station, the one with the "76" sign in Chinese on the corner of Pacific and Taylor. His uncle had Zeke do the detail work, the shine and buff, and now he still calls Zeke the "Detail Man." Some guys still call him Detail, but I like to call him Zeke. His mother'd asked a nurse at Chinese Hospital to give him an American name. Ezekiel was what he got. A spit-quick kind of name. I thought it was perfect; Zeke was a short man with a short temper.

From *Bone*
By Fae Myenne Ng

1. What did Zeke do at his uncle's gas station?

   _____

A possible answer is, *He used to hang around there and shine and buff cars*. The writer shows you a picture of a boy who works at an early age at a family business.

2. How do you know that Zeke's family is Chinese?

   _____

A possible answer is, *The "76" sign is in Chinese*.

3. Why does Zeke's uncle still call him "the Detail Man?"

   _____

You may have written something like, *Zeke's uncle appreciates and respects Zeke's skill*.

A. Read the fiction passage below.

"And looky here—you drop that school, you hear? I'll learn people to bring up a boy to put on airs over his own father and let on to be better'n what *he* is. You lemme catch you fooling around that school again, you hear? Your mother couldn't read, and she couldn't write, nuther, before she died. None of the family
5 couldn't, before *they* died. I can't; and here you're a-swelling yourself up like this. I ain't the man to stand it—you hear? Say—lemme hear you read."

I took up a book and begun something about General Washington and the wars. When I'd read about a half a minute, he fetched the book a whack with his hand and knocked it across the house. He says:

10 "It's so. You can do it. I had my doubts when you told me. Now looky here; you stop that putting on frills. I won't have it. I'll lay for you, my smarty; and if I catch you about that school I'll tan you good. First you know you'll get religion, too. I never see such a son."

From *The Adventures of Huckleberry Finn*
By Mark Twain

B. Choose the best answer, and write it on the line.

Example:

Based on the way he speaks, do you think this man has a formal education?

No, because he says things like "looky here" and "I'll learn people" instead of "Look here"
and "I'll teach people."

1. What does the character say to make you think this is a father talking to a son?

_____

2. What does the boy do that shows he doesn't want to disobey the man?

_____

C. Complete each sentence with one of the two choices in parentheses.

3. This man thinks that education is _____ . (*important* or *unnecessary*)

4. This man thinks his son is getting too _____ . (*civilized* or *wild*)

Answers and explanations start on page 108.

Point of View

The writer tells the story from a certain perspective, or **point of view.** The most direct point of view is first-person narrative. In **first-person narrative,** the character calls him- or herself "I." There are two other points of view, that of another character in the story and that of someone outside the story. When you read the passage below, look for point of view.

EXAMPLE

I was getting along fine with Mama, Papa-Daddy and Uncle Rondo until my sister Stella-Rondo just separated from her husband and came back home again. Mr. Whitaker! Of course I went with Mr. Whitaker first, when he first appeared here in China Grove, taking "Pose Yourself" photos, and Stella-Rondo broke us up. Told him I was one sided. Bigger on one side than the other, which is a deliberate, calculated falsehood: I'm the same. Stella-Rondo is exactly twelve months to the day younger than I am and for that reason she's spoiled.

From "Why I Live at the P.O."
By Eudora Welty

1. In what point of view is this paragraph written?

_____

You probably said *first-person narrative*. The character calls herself "I."

2. The paragraph on page 40 is about Zeke, a character in the story. Does it seem as if the narrator is in the story?

_____

A possible answer is *no; the narrator is probably outside the story.*

3. Which point of view do you prefer, the one used above or the one used on page 40? Why?

_____

Possible answers: *the one used above because I feel closer to this character* or *the one used on page 40 because I have a better picture of the other characters in the story.*

4. Write something that Stella-Rondo might say in response to the paragraph above. Use the first person-narrative.

_____

_____

Possible answer: *My sister is a liar. I never wanted any of her boyfriends, and I'm not spoiled. At least I tried to make my own life. She still lives with Mama. And Mr. Whitaker broke up with her because he got tired of her complaining, not because of anything I said.*

A. Read the fiction passage below.

"I don't know why I was so impressed. Perhaps because you were the first boy who ever paid much attention to me."

He did not like to hear this. He remembered how concerned he had been that she might be seeing somebody else. Now she made it sound as though nobody

5 else wanted her. "India, stop this nonsense. I could recall offhand the names of several young men who found you extremely attractive."

For a little while she was quiet. She appeared to be thinking. Then she said, "Walter, tell me the truth. Did you find me attractive?"

He frowned. "What on earth has gotten into you? All at once for no good reason

10 you behave as if—I don't know what. You were an attractive girl and you are today an attractive woman."

"Am I?"

"You are indeed."

She looked at him playfully. "Would it hurt so much to tell me once in a while?"

"I'm afraid I'm not good at that sort of business."

From *Mr. Bridge*
By Evan S. Connell

B. Check off the best answer.

1. In this passage, how does Connell develop these characters?

   ❑ action   ❑ dialogue

2. Which word below best describes Walter?

   ❑ stern   ❑ needy   ❑ strange

C. Write each answer on the line.

3. Is this story told in the first-person narrative (from the "I" point of view)?

   _____

4. From the story, you learn that India's character wants Walter to tell her that she is

   _____ .

Answers and explanations start on page 108.

"The grandmother didn't want to go to Florida. 'I wouldn't take my children in any direction with a criminal like that aloose in it.'"

Telling the Story

Sequence of Events

In the video, you learned that the **sequence of events** is the order in which things happen. To figure out the sequence of events, you need to focus on each individual event.

In the first sentence of the example below, the first event is "go across the field to Fred Brightleaf's." You can look at the *Sequence Diagram* on page 119 to see some other events from the example. In the example below, the events are underlined.

EXAMPLE

That afternoon, as soon as I could escape attention, I knew I would <u>go across the field to Fred Brightleaf's.</u> Fred and I would <u>catch Rufus Brightleaf's past-work old draft horse, Prince, and ride him over to the pond for a swim.</u> And after supper, when Grandma and Grandpa would be content just to sit on the front porch in the dark, and you could feel the place growing lonesome for other times, I would <u>drift away down to the little house</u> beside the woods where Dick Watson and Aunt Sarah Jane lived. While the light drained from the sky and night fell I would <u>sit with Dick on the rock steps</u> in front of the door and <u>listen to him</u> tell of the horses and mules and foxhounds he remembered.

From *A World Lost*
By Wendell Berry

1. What is the correct order of events?
    a. go across the field to Fred Brightleaf's
    b. sit with Dick on the rock steps
    c. drift away down to the little house
    d. catch Rufus Brightleaf's past-work old draft horse, Prince, and ride him over to the pond for a swim

The correct order is: *a, d, c, b.*

To find the order of events, you can often use time clues such as *that afternoon* and *after supper.*

2. The last thing the narrator did in this imagined afternoon is _____.

You probably said *sit with Dick on the rock steps and listen to him.* That is the last action in the passage.

See the *Sequence Diagram* on page 119.

A. Read the fiction passage below.

Back at the house she laid down the baby for his nap, then carefully washed the produce and put it in the refrigerator, all the while feeling her mother's eyes on her hands. "The worst thing for you," she kept repeating under her breath until she annoyed herself. She moved around the edges of the rooms as though her
5 big mother and demanding grandmother were still there taking up most of the space; the house felt both empty and cramped at the same time, and Lou Ann felt a craving for something she couldn't put a finger on, maybe some kind of food she had eaten a long time ago. She opened the curtains in the front room to let in the light. The sky was hard and bright, not a blue sky full of water. Strangely
10 enough, it still surprised her sometimes to open that window and not see Kentucky.

From *The Bean Trees*
By Barbara Kingsolver

B. Write *Yes* if word or phrase is an event; write *No* if it is not.

Example:

<u>Yes</u>   "laid down the baby"

<u>No</u>   "blue sky full of water"

Laid down the baby is an event, but a *blue sky full of water* is not an event.

_____ **1.** "carefully washed the produce"
_____ **2.** "kind of food"
_____ **3.** "moved around the edges"
_____ **4.** "Kentucky"

C. Answer the question; then put the events in the proper order. The first event has already been done for you.

5. What word in the first line helps you determine the order of events?

_____

<u>1</u> **6.** "laid down the baby"
_____ "opened the curtains in the front room"
_____ "put it in the refrigerator"
_____ "washed the produce"

Answers and explanations start on page 109.

Conflict

Conflict is a struggle that can be within a character, between characters, or between a character and an outside force.

Most of the conflict in the passage below is between two characters, Lena and Milkman. They're arguing about someone named Corinthians, who has been dating a certain man. Some of the conflict, however, is within Milkman himself. He has a secret, and he can't explain his attitude to Lena. See page 120 for a *Story Map*.

EXAMPLE

"I know you told Daddy about Corinthians, that she was seeing a man. Secretly. And—"

"I *had* to. I'd love for her to find somebody, but I *know* that man. I—I've been around him. And I don't think he . . ." Milkman stopped, unable to explain. About the Days, about what he suspected.

"Oh?" Her voice was thick with sarcasm. "You have somebody else in mind for her?"

"No."

"No? But he's Southside, and not good enough for her? It's good enough for you, but not for her, right?"

"Lena . . ."

"What do you know about somebody not being good enough for somebody else? And since when did you care whether Corinthians stood up or fell down?"

From *Song of Solomon*
By Toni Morrison

1. Which line shows a conflict within Milkman?

_____

You probably chose this line: *"Milkman stopped, unable to explain. About the Days, about what he suspected."*

2. Which line is the first to show conflict between Milkman and Lena?

_____

You probably chose this line: *"Her voice was thick with sarcasm."*

See the *Story Map* on page 120.

A. Read the fiction passage below.

The day after his termination there were unemployment benefits to see about.
He went downtown to the state office to fill out papers and look for another
job. But there were no jobs in his line of work, or in any other line of work. His
face began to sweat as he tried to describe to Sandy the milling crowd of men

5 and women down there. That evening he got back on the sofa. He began
spending all of his time there, as if, she thought, it was the thing he was supposed
to do now that he no longer had any work. Once in a while he had to go talk to
somebody about a job possibility, and every two weeks he had to go sign
something to collect his unemployment compensation. But the rest of the time

10 he stayed on the sofa. It's like he *lives* there, Sandy thought.

From "Preservation" in *Cathedral*
By Raymond Carver

B. Write the letter of the answer on the line.

_____ **1.** Which of these is a conflict between the character and an outside force?
    a. He is fired and faces unemployment.
    b. He's sweating as he tries to talk about the crowd.
    c. Sandy thinks he "lives" on the sofa.

_____ **2.** Most of the passage shows conflict
    a. within a character
    b. between characters
    c. between a character and an outside force

C. Write the answer on the lines.

3. If a conflict developed between these two characters in the next paragraph, what
would the struggle probably be about? Explain.

_____

_____

_____

4. If there's conflict within Sandy, what might it be about?

_____

_____

Answers and explanations start on page 109.

READING SKILLS

Answering Special Synthesis Questions

On the GED Reading Test, there are some questions that require you to make connections between the passage that you read and additional information that you are provided in the question. These are called **special synthesis questions.** To answer these questions, read the information before the question, and think about how it relates to the topic of the paragraph. The example below uses the selection by Mark Twain on page 41.

EXAMPLE

"I'll learn people to bring up a boy to put on airs over his own father and let on to be better'n what *he* is. You lemme catch you fooling around that school again, you hear? Your mother couldn't read, and she couldn't write, nuther, before she died. None of the family couldn't, before *they* died. I can't; and here you're a-swelling yourself up like this." ◄── passage

1. In a speech titled "Advice to Youth" given in 1882, Mark Twain said, "Always obey your parents. When they are present. This is the best policy in the long run. Because if you don't, they will make you. Most parents think they know better than you do, and you can generally make more by humoring that superstition than you can by acting on your own better judgment." ◄── question introduction with new information

    Based on the passage and the information above, which of these statements ◄── question would Mark Twain most likely agree with?

    (1) Children cannot be trusted to make their own decisions.

    (2) Parents always know better than children.

    (3) Children should always do what their parents tell them to do.

    (4) Some children are smarter than their parents and can outsmart them.

    (5) Parents should physically force their children into following instructions

The correct answer is option (**4**) **Some children are smarter than their parents and can outsmart them.** The passage establishes that Huck is exhibiting his intelligence, and the quoted speech sets out how children can use their "smarts" to outwit their parents.

- **What do the passage and question introduction have in common?**
- **Read the passage with the question in mind.** Do you see a connection? What is it?
- **Think through the choices.** Only option (4) makes the connection.

TEST-TAKING HINTS

- Think about the main point of the new information provided by the question.
- Review the passage with that point in mind.
- Find the answer choice that best reflects that connection.

Sample GED Question

Elsewhere in the novel, Huck realizes he's not scared of his father anymore. "I reckoned I was scared now, too; but in a minute I see I was mistaken. That is, after the first jolt . . . I see I warn't scared of him worth bothering about."

What probably happened to change Huck's attitude?

(1) He got older and understood more.

(2) He realized he was just like his father.

(3) His father got weaker.

(4) His father was nicer to him now.

(5) He was more afraid of his foster mother, Widow Douglas.

You can eliminate options (4) and (5) because they don't make sense with this passage or the previous one. Neither (2) nor (3) seem to be true. Only **(1)** is reasonable.

GED TEST-TAKING SKILL PRACTICE

ANSWERING GED QUESTIONS

Questions 1 and 2 are based on the passage below.

John does not know how much I really suffer. He knows there is no reason to suffer, and that satisfies him. Of course it is only nervousness. It does weigh on me so not to do my duty in any way! I meant to be such a help to John, such a real rest and comfort, and here I am a comparative burden
5 already! Nobody would believe what an effort it is to do what little I am able,—to dress and entertain, and order things. It is fortunate Mary is so good with the baby. Such a dear baby! And yet I cannot be with him, it makes me so nervous. I suppose John never was nervous in his life.

From *The Yellow Wallpaper*
By Charlotte Perkins Gilman

1. Earlier in the story, the narrator tells us that John "scoffs openly at any talk of things not to be felt and seen and put down in figures."

   What might this information and the passage above suggest about the narrator's condition?

   Her condition is

   (1) very serious

   (2) not very serious

   (3) all in her mind

   (4) a physical problem

   (5) easily treatable

2. Gilman suffered from a form of depression similar to the narrator's. She helped herself recover through her creative writing.

   Based on this information, what might Gilman recommend the narrator do?

   (1) get plenty of rest

   (2) take whatever medication she was given

   (3) be more like her husband, John

   (4) find some sort of creative outlet

   (5) entertain more often

   Answers and explanations start on page 109.

Journal Writing About Fiction

When you read something that interests you or makes you think, you can write about it in a journal. A journal can be a notebook that you write in from time to time, when the mood strikes you. When you write in a journal, you write just for you. It's you talking to yourself on paper.

EXAMPLE

Here's a journal entry about the main character in the paragraph from "Why I Live at the P.O.," on page 42.

> I was getting along fine with Mama, Papa-Daddy and Uncle Rondo until my sister Stella-Rondo just separated from her husband and came back home again.
> Mr. Whitaker!

> I like the character because she seems real, and she's funny.
>
> I didn't like all the names because I got confused.
>
> I was frustrated by not knowing why she says "Mr. Whitaker!"

Here's a sample journal entry about the setting in the paragraph from *The Big Sleep,* on page 39.

> It opened into a sort of vestibule that was about as warm as a slow oven. He came in after me, shut the outer door, opened an inner door and we went through that. Then it was really hot. The air was thick, wet, steamy, and larded with the cloying smell of tropical orchids in bloom.

> I like the way the air gets thick and hot and too-sweet smelling when the narrator goes farther into the house. It reminded me of the greenhouse I used to visit when I was a kid. It was always warm and humid in the greenhouse, and it had a unique smell. It had several rooms and the last room was the desert room. So the farther you went into the greenhouse, the warmer it got, just like in this passage. That's how I pictured the place the narrator was walking into. It's interesting—the things you remember sometimes.

JOURNAL-WRITING HINTS

- Write about an event or a character, place, or story that creates a strong feeling in you.
- Write easily and informally—just get your ideas down.
- Don't worry about mistakes. Remember, your journal is just for you.

A. Reread the passage on page 47. Use the questions below to brainstorm a sample journal entry.

What did you like about this passage?

_____

_____

_____

What did you not like about this passage?

_____

_____

_____

What frustrated you about the conflict
between Sandy and the unemployed man?

_____

_____

_____

B. In a journal, write one or two paragraphs that bring together your answers above.

C. Self-Check List

How did you like writing about this fiction passage?_____

_____

_____

Did you think it's something you would do again?_____

_____

_____

Did you learn something? What?_____

_____

_____

Which writing hint was the most helpful to you? Why?_____

_____

_____

Answers and explanations start on page 109.

GED Review: Fiction

Choose the <u>one best answer</u> to the questions below.

<u>Questions 1 through 3</u> refer to the following passage.

WHY IS THIS MAN EMBARRASED?

The man asked, "Can we git some water, ma'am?"

A look of annoyance crossed Mae's face. "Sure, go ahead." She said softly
5 over her shoulder, "I'll keep my eye on the hose." She watched while the man slowly unscrewed the radiator cap and ran the hose in.

A woman in the car, a flaxen-haired
10 woman, said, "See if you can't git it here."

The man turned off the hose and screwed on the cap again. The little boys took the hose from him and they
15 upended it and drank thirstily. The man took off his dark, stained hat and stood with a curious humility in front of the screen. "Could you see your way to sell us a loaf of bread, ma'am?"

20 Mae said, "This ain't a grocery store. We got bread to make san'widges."

"I know, ma'am." His humility was insistent. "We need bread and there ain't nothin' for quite a piece, they say."

25 " 'F we sell bread we gonna run out." Mae's tone was faltering.

"We're hungry," the man said.

"Whyn't you buy a san'widge? We got nice san'widges, hamburgs."

30 "We'd sure admire to do that, ma'am. But we can't. We got to make a dime do all of us." And he said embarrassedly, "We ain't got but a little."

Mae said, "You can't get no loaf of
35 bread for a dime. We only got fifteen-cent loafs."

From behind her Al growled, "God Almighty, Mae, give 'em bread."

From *The Grapes of Wrath*
By John Steinbeck

1. What is the mood of this paragraph?
    (1) bored
    (2) funny
    (3) pitiful
    (4) joyful
    (5) angry

2. Which is the conflict between a character and an outside force?
    (1) poverty and the man
    (2) Mae and the man
    (3) flaxen-haired woman and the man
    (4) little boys and the man
    (5) the man and his embarrassment

3. Which is the first event?
    (1) The boys drink thirstily.
    (2) Mae offers to sell the man sandwiches.
    (3) The man asks if he can buy bread.
    (4) The man turns off the hose.
    (5) Mae refuses to sell the bread.

WHAT DOES THIS BOY BELIEVE?

Jerome worshipped his father: the verb is exact. As man re-creates God, so Jerome re-created his father—from a restless widowed author into a
5 mysterious adventurer who travelled in far places—Nice, Beirut, Majorca, even the Canaries. The time had arrived about his eighth birthday when Jerome believed that his father either
10 "ran guns" or was a member of the British Secret Service. Now it occurred to him that his father might have been wounded in "a hail of machine-gun bullets."

15 Mr. Wordsworth played with the ruler on his desk. He seemed at a loss how to continue. He said, "You knew your father was in Naples?"

"Yes, sir."

20 "Your aunt heard from the hospital today."

"Oh."

Mr. Wordsworth said with desperation, "It was a street accident."

25 "Yes, sir?" It seemed quite likely to Jerome that they would call it a street accident. The police, of course, had fired first; his father would not take human life except as a last resort.

30 "I'm afraid your father was very seriously hurt indeed."

"Oh."

"In fact, Jerome, he died yesterday. Quite without pain."

35 "Did they shoot him through the heart?"

"I beg your pardon. What did you say, Jerome?"

"Did they shoot him through the heart?"

"Nobody shot him, Jerome. A pig fell
40 on him."

From "A Shocking Accident"
By Graham Greene

4. Where does this scene take place?
   (1) Nice
   (2) British Secret Service Headquarters
   (3) Naples
   (4) Mr. Wordsworth's office
   (5) a barnyard

5. Who is telling the story?
   (1) the pig
   (2) Jerome
   (3) Mr. Wordsworth
   (4) someone outside the story
   (5) Jerome's father

6. Which information tells you the most about Jerome?
   (1) what he says
   (2) what he thinks
   (3) what Mr. Wordsworth says
   (4) what Mr. Wordsworth does
   (5) what happens to his father

Answers and explanations start on page 110.

GED REVIEW

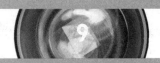
Poetry

LESSON GOALS

READING SKILLS

- Read poetry
- Hear and see the poem
- Get the message

GED TEST-TAKING SKILLS

- Using purpose questions and line numbers

READING & WRITING CONNECTION

- Poetry starters

GED REVIEW

1. Think About the Topic

In this program, you will practice answering questions based on poetry selections. Poetry is literature that is much more expressive than regular fiction. Poetry allows the writer a lot of freedom in word choice, rhythm, and rhyme. As Sonya Sanchez says in the video, "Each line is like a chapter . . . each line has the power." On the test, you will read a poem and answer multiple-choice questions about it. You'll use poetry skills such as "hearing and seeing" the poem, identifying the speaker, and getting the message.

To help you understand poetry, this program will introduce you to several different people. Former U.S. poet laureate Robert Pinsky will talk about his *Favorite Poems Project,* and you will hear from two of the participants in this project about their favorite poems. You will also meet a GED teacher and a GED graduate, who will discuss favorite poems of theirs, as well as teach you a little about the style and structure of poetry.

2. Prepare to Watch the Video

Do you like poems? Why or why not? _____

_____

Have you ever written a poem? _____

Did you write the poem for a school assignment or for your own personal expression? _____

_____

3. Preview the Questions

Read the questions under *Think About the Program,* and keep them in mind as you watch the program. You will review them after you watch.

4. Study the Vocabulary

Review the terms to the right. Understanding the meaning of key poetry vocabulary will help you understand the video and the rest of this lesson.

WATCH THE PROGRAM

As you watch the program, pay special attention to the host who introduces or summarizes major poetry ideas that you need to learn about. The host will also give you important information about the GED Reading Test.

AFTER YOU WATCH

1. Think About the Program

What is the point of figurative language in poems? For example what is the difference between "cold" and "blue black cold"?

Which do you prefer to read, poetry or stories? Why?

Do you like poetry with regular rhythm and rhyme like the Frost poem? Or do you prefer irregular rhythm and rhyme like the poem by Robert Hayden, "Those Winter Sundays"?

Which poem from the program did you like the best? Why?

2. Make the Connection

If you wrote a poem, what would the first image be? Close your eyes, and wait until a sense image comes. It could start with a smell, a sight, or a sound. Write one line. See how it makes you feel. Now read it aloud.

TERMS

figurative language— creative language that goes beyond literal meaning

line—the basic unit of poetry; a word or group of words in a row

literal language—factual language that has no alternative meaning

metaphor—figurative language that compares two unlike things using the word *is*

personification—metaphor that gives human traits to nonhuman objects

rhyme—two or more end sounds that are the same

rhythm—pattern of sounds

simile—figurative language that uses the words *like* or *as*

speaker—who or what is saying the words in a poem

stanza—group of lines in a poem usually separated by a line space

theme—the meaning, or message, of a poem

tone—overall feeling of a poem

"Read the poem aloud a couple of times, not thinking about the meaning at all."

Reading Poetry

Reading Lines of Poetry

In the video, you heard poetry read aloud. In this lesson, you will learn to read and understand poems. Reading poetry is different from reading other types of writing because you read lines (instead of sentences) and stanzas (instead of paragraphs).

The most basic unit of poetry is a **line.** It may contain a sentence, a part of a sentence, a sentence fragment (a group of words, not a correct sentence), or even just a word. A complete idea in a poem may be chopped up by **line breaks.** The line breaks give poetry its special feel and are important to reading the poem, but you need to read across the line breaks to understand the poem's meaning. Read the poem below:

EXAMPLE

> The night is too long to the sleepless.
> The road is too long to the footsore.
> Life is too long to a woman
> Made foolish by passion.
> Why did I find a crooked guide
> On the twisted paths of love?
>
> "LV"
> From *The Love Poems of Marichiko*
> By Marichiko, translated by Kenneth Rexroth

To understand the poem, you should use the punctuation to group ideas together into sentences or complete thoughts. The slash (/) shows where the poem has line breaks.

> The night is too long to the sleepless. /
> The road is too long to the footsore. /
> Life is too long to a woman / made foolish by passion. /
> Why did I find a crooked guide / on the twisted paths of love?

1. Ignoring the line breaks, how many sentences are in the poem "LV"? _____

Once the lines of the poem are organized, you can see that there are *four sentences.*

2. How many line breaks did you have to "go across" to read the sentences?_____

You had to go across *two* line breaks to create two complete thoughts.

3. Which lines tell you different things that are too long? _____

The *first, second, and third lines* tell you that the night, the road, and life can be too long.

A. Read the poem aloud and then silently. Go back and put slash marks (/) at the end of each sentence or complete thought, and read it a third time.

It was a picture I had after the war.
A bombed English church. I was too young
to know the word *English* or *war,*
but I knew the picture.
5 The ruined city still seemed noble.
The cathedral with its roof blown off
was not less godly. The church was the same
plus rain and sky. Birds flew in and out
of the holes God's fist made in the walls.
10 All our desire for love or children
is treated like rags by the enemy.
I knew so much and sang anyway.
Like a bird who will sing until
it is brought down. When they take
15 away the trees, the child picks up a stick
and says, this is a tree, this the house
and the family. As we might. Through a door
of what had been a house, into the field
of rubble, walks a single lamb, tilting
20 its head, curious, unafraid, hungry.

"The Lamb"
From *Chosen by the Lion*
By Linda Gregg

B. Write the answers to each question.

1. Write the first three complete ideas on the lines below as separate sentences or sentence fragments.

_____

_____

2. How many slash marks did you put in the poem? (How many ideas were there?)

_____

C. Read the following ideas from the poem, and write what you think each means.

All our desire for love or children
is treated like rags by the enemy.

3. _____

Answers and explanations start on page 110.

Reading Stanzas

A **stanza** is a group of lines in a poem that are separated by a space. Stanzas are used to organize related ideas in poems, just as paragraphs are used in prose fiction and nonfiction.

As you read the poem, think about the **speaker**—that is, who or what is saying the words in a poem. In the poem below, the speaker is 20 years old (the poet uses the term *score,* which means 20 years) and figures to live 50 more years. Notice how each stanza contains its own idea.

EXAMPLE

Loveliest of trees, the cherry now
Is hung with bloom along the bough,
And stands about the woodland ride
Wearing white for Eastertide.

Now, of my threescore years and ten,
Twenty will not come again,
And take from seventy springs a score,
It only leaves me fifty more.

And since to look at things in bloom
Fifty springs are little room,
About the woodlands I will go
To see the cherry hung with snow.

"Loveliest of Trees"
From *A Shropshire Lad*
By A. E. Housman

1.   How many lines are in each stanza?_____

You should have written *four.* Each group is made up of four lines.

2.   How many stanzas does this poem have?_____

You should have written *three.* There are three separate groups of lines in this poem.

3.   With what word does the second stanza begin? _____

You probably wrote *Now.* The second stanza begins after the first line space.

4.   Which stanza contains the line *Wearing white for Eastertide?* _____

You probably said *the first stanza.* The first group of lines contains the Eastertide phrase.

A. Read the poem out loud to yourself. Then read it again silently, and answer the questions below.

The sea rocks her thousands of waves.
The sea is divine.
Hearing the loving sea
I rock my son.

The wind wandering by night
rocks the wheat.
Hearing the loving wind
I rock my son.

God, the Father, soundlessly rocks
His thousands of worlds.
Feeling His hand in the shadow
I rock my son.

"Rocking"
From *Selected Poems of Gabriela Mistral: A Bilingual Edition*
By Gabriela Mistral, translated by Doris Dana

B. Write the correct answer in the blank.

1. How many stanzas are in "Rocking?" _____

2. What two words begin the second stanza? _____

3. How many lines are in the third stanza? _____

4. How many sentences are in the third stanza? _____

5. What phrase is repeated at the end of each stanza? _____

_____

6. Who is the speaker in the poem?

   a. the sea   **b.** a mother

C. Match each stanza with its meaning.

____ **7.** stanza 1   **a.** I rock my son as God rocks the worlds.

____ **8.** stanza 2   **b.** I rock my son as the sea rocks the waves.

____ **9.** stanza 3   **c.** I rock my son as the wind rocks the wheat.

Answers and explanations start on page 111.

"Don't be so mean man unless you mean to be mean   mean   mean mean."

Hearing and Seeing the Poem

Rhyme, Repetition, and Rhythm

In the video, you learned about rhyme, repetition, and rhythm. In the quote above, you see the repetition, using the same word or sound, of *mean.* This creates a steady pushing **rhythm.** The rhythm in a poem is a pattern of sounds.

As you know, poems sometimes have **rhymes,** ending sounds of two words that are the same. When this occurs at the end of two lines of poetry, it is called **end rhyme.** You will see an example of end rhyme in the poem below.

EXAMPLE

Four be the things I am wiser to know:
Idleness, sorrow, a friend, and a foe.

Four be the things I'd been better without:
Love, curiosity, freckles, and doubt.

Three be the things I shall never attain:
Envy, content, and sufficient champagne.

Three be the things I shall have till I die:
Laughter and hope and a sock in the eye.

"Inventory"
By Dorothy Parker

As you can see, the last word of each stanza rhymes—for example, *know* and *foe.* This poem also has a rhythm. Did you notice yourself reading the poem a certain way? The rhythm of each stanza is: *long - short short, long short, short; long - short, short, long.* Rhythm is created by the word choice and rhyme pattern that the poet uses.

1.   What are the two words that rhyme in stanza 2? _____

The words are *without* and *doubt.* Both words end with the sound of *out.*

2.   What six words are repeated at the begining of stanzas 3 and 4? Is the rhythm of these lines the same?

_____

The repeated words are *Three be the things I shall.* Notice that all of the lines in the poem have the same rhythm.

A. Read the poem below.

I will arise and go now, and go to Innisfree,
And a small cabin build there, of clay and wattles[1] made:
Nine bean-rows will I have there, a hive for the honeybee,
And live alone in the bee-loud glade.[2]

5 And I shall have some peace there, for peace comes dropping slow,
Dropping from the veils of the morning to where the cricket sings;
There midnight's all a glimmer, and noon a purple glow,
And evening full of the linnet's[3] wings.

I will arise and go now, for always night and day
10 I hear lake water lapping with low sounds by the shore;
While I stand on the roadway, or on the pavements grey,
I hear it in the deep heart's core.

[1] sticks   [2] an open space in a wood or forest   [3] a type of bird

"The Lake Isle of Innisfree"
By William Butler Yeats

B. Write the word from the poem that rhymes with each of the words below. Then give that word's line number.

Example:
made   word   _glade_   line _4_

Reason: The word *made* rhymes with *glade* in Line 4

1. sings   word _____   line _____

2. shore   word _____   line _____

C. Answer the questions below.

3. What phrase from stanza 1 repeats in stanza 3? _____

4. What word repeats in line 5? _____

5. What phrase from line 10 repeats in line 12? _____

6. Read line 12 and listen to the rhythm. Is it the same as the rhythm in line 4?

_____

Answers and explanations start on page 111.

Figurative Language

Literal language is straightforward, factual language. It's the way you express yourself every day. **Figurative language** is creative language that goes beyond literal meaning. There are three main types of figurative language: simile, metaphor, and personification:

- **Simile**—figurative language that compares two unlike things using *like* or *as*
  Example: "My love is <u>like</u> a red, red rose."
  Here love is compared to a rose. The two things are similar, yet unlike.

- **Metaphor**—figurative language that compares two unlike things using *is*
  Example: "He <u>is</u> a snake."
  Here a man is spoken of as if he were a snake.

- **Personification**—a type of metaphor that gives human qualities to nonhuman objects.
  Example: "The shadows danced slowly in the moonlight."
  Here shadows are given the human ability to dance.

Look for examples of figurative language in the poem below.

EXAMPLE

    Fear passes from man to man
    Unknowing,
    As one leaf passes its shudder
    To another.

5 All at once the whole tree is trembling
    And there is no sign of the wind.

    "Fear"
    By Charles Simic

Mark each example with an *M* if it is a metaphor, an *S* if it is a simile, a *P* if it is an example of personification, or an *L* if it is literal language.

_____ **1.** "All at once the whole tree is trembling"

_____ **2.** "And there is no sign of the wind."

You probably marked the phrase 1 *P* because the tree is said to tremble as a man would when afraid. You probably marked phrase 2 *L* because it is literal language.

3. Which word in stanza 1 lets you know there is a simile in that stanza? _____

You probably said *As*. The word *as* is one signal for a simile. Here the passing of fear from one man to another is being compared to leaves shuddering on a tree.

A. Read the poem below.

The D is desperate.
The B wants to take a vacation,
live on a billboard, be broad and brave.
The E is mad at the R for upstaging him.
5 The little c wants to be a big C if possible,
and the P pauses long between thoughts.

How much better to be a story, story.
Can you read me?

We have to live on this white board
10 together like a neighborhood.
We would rather be the tail of a cloud,
one letter becoming another,
or lost in a boy's pocket
shapeless as lint,
15 the same boy who squints to read us
believing we convey a secret message.
  Be *his* friend.
We are so tired of meaning nothing.

"Eye Test"
By Naomi Shihab Nye

B. Next to each letter, choose the human trait the poet has given it.

Example:

 P *has thoughts on*

Reason: P takes a pause between thoughts. That's a human trait.

_____ **1.** D	**a.** ambition
_____ **2.** little c	**b.** anger
_____ **3.** E	**c.** desperation

C. Write what the letters are being compared to in each line.

 4. line 10 _____

 5. line 14 _____

Answers and explanations start on page 111.

"I felt it represented the passage of time and growing up."

Getting the Message

Understanding the Tone

Above is a quote from the video about the message of the Robert Frost poem on page 67. The idea of "growing up" is supported by the poem's **tone** — its attitude or overall feeling.

What is the attitude of the poem below? Read the poem aloud.

E X A M P L E

> The tusks that clashed in mighty brawls
> Of mastodons,¹ are billiard balls.
>
> The sword of Charlemagne the Just
> Is ferric oxide, known as rust.
>
> The grizzly bear whose potent hug
> Was feared by all, is now a rug.
>
> Great Caesar's bust is on the shelf,
> And I don't feel so well myself.
>
> ¹ prehistoric elephants
>
> "On the Vanity of Earthly Greatness"
> By Arthur Guiterman

1. What became of the mastodons' tusks in line 2? What tone does this develop?

_____

You may have answered, *They became billiard balls.* Billiard balls were once made of ivory, from elephant tusks. The speaker's tone is ironic. You wouldn't expect mighty animals to end up as billiard balls.

2. What does the last line mean? What does the speaker's attitude seem to be?

_____

_____

You may have said something like, *The speaker knows that, like all the other things mentioned in the poem, he won't live forever. The speaker seems to be laughing at life.*

3. In a word, what is the attitude of this poem? _____

You probably said *humorous.* The poem reminds us not to take life too seriously.

A. Read the poem below.

When I came back, he was gone.
My mother was in the bathroom
crying, my sister in her crib
restless but asleep. The sun
5 was shining in the bay window,
the grass had just been cut.
No one mentioned the other woman,
nights he spent in that stranger's house.

I sat at my desk and wrote him a note.
10 When my mother saw his name on the sheet
of paper, she asked me to leave the house.
When she spoke, her voice was like a whisper
to someone else, her hand a weight
on my arm I could not feel.

15 In the evening, though, I opened the door
and saw a thousand houses just like ours.
I thought I was the one who was leaving,
and behind me I heard my mother's voice
asking me to stay. But I was thirteen
20 and wishing I were a man I listened
to no one, and no words from a woman
I loved were strong enough to make me stop.

"My Father's Leaving"
By Ira Sadoff

B. Answer the questions below.

1. What is the speaker's attitude in the last two lines, as he remembers his
   thirteen-year-old self? _____

2. What is the tone of this poem? _____
   a. excitement
   b. grief
   c. restlessness

C. Write five words or phrases from the poem that help create the poem's tone.

3. _____

Answers and explanations start on page 111.

Reading for Theme

Theme is the message of the poem. The message is different from the tone. For example, the tone of the poem on page 64 is humorous, but its theme is that physical power doesn't last.

EXAMPLE

How do I love thee? Let me count the ways.
I love thee to the depth and breadth and height
My soul can reach, when feeling out of sight
For the ends of Being and ideal Grace.
5 I love thee to the level of everyday's
Most quiet need, by sun and candle-light.
I love thee freely, as men strive for Right;
I love thee purely, as they turn from Praise.
I love thee with the passion put to use
10 In my old griefs, and with my childhood's faith.
I love thee with a love I seemed to lose
With my lost saints,—I love thee with the breath,
Smiles, tears, of all my life!—and, if God choose,
I shall but love thee better after death.

"Sonnet 43"
By Elizabeth Barrett Browning

1. Which line shows the speaker's love is forever? _____

You probably said, *line 14*. The speaker says that her love will continue even after death.

2. Which line shows that the speaker loves all day and all night? _____

You probably said, *line 6*. Sun identifies day; candlelight identifies night.

3. How does the first line make the message seem more personal?

_____

You probably said something like, *Line 1 seems to respond to her lover's question.* It's as if the speaker just heard someone ask, "How do you love me?"

4. What is the overall message of the poem?

_____

A reasonable answer is, *She loves him in all ways and forever.*

A. Read the poem below.

Whose woods these are I think I know.
His house is in the village, though;
He will not see me stopping here
To watch his woods fill up with snow.

5 My little horse must think it queer
To stop without a farmhouse near
Between the woods and frozen lake
The darkest evening of the year.

He gives his harness bells a shake
10 To ask if there is some mistake.
The only other sound's the sweep
Of easy wind and downy flake.

The woods are lovely, dark, and deep,
But I have promises to keep,
15 And miles to go before I sleep,
And miles to go before I sleep.

"Stopping by Woods on a Snowy Evening"
By Robert Frost

B. Answer the questions about the poem.

1. What is the speaker's attitude in lines 3 and 4? _____
   a. hopeful
   b. secretive

2. What is the overall message of the poem? _____
   a. Take responsibility in life.
   b. Try to get out of your obligations.

C. Write the answers on the lines.

3. What does the last stanza show you about the speaker?

_____

4. How does the speaker's attitude change from the first stanza to the last?
How does this affect the theme?

_____

5. Explain how the poem establishes its theme.

_____

Answers and explanations start on page 111.

Using Purpose Questions and Line Numbers

On the GED Reading Test, you will see a question above the selection you are going to read. It's not a title; it is a **purpose question**—a question for you to think about as you read. You do not have to provide an answer to this question.

As you read the selection, you will see **line numbers** to the left of the passage. The numbers appear every five lines and can help you find the answer you're looking for. Here's an example that uses Charles Simic's poem "Fear," from page 62.

EXAMPLE

HOW DOES THIS SPEAKER PICTURE FEAR? ◄─── | Purpose Question

Fear passes from man to man
Unknowing,
As one leaf passes its shudder
To another. ─────── | Line Number

5 All at once the whole tree is trembling
And there is no sign of the wind.

What does fear look like to the speaker in line 5?

(1) like the wind
(2) like a shuddering leaf
(3) like a trembling tree
(4) like a man looking at another man
(5) like a tree that is still

The correct answer is **(3) like a trembling tree.** This answer is correct because it is in line 5, and it tells what fear looks like to the speaker. The other choices are not in line 5, even though they are part of the picture of fear.

What does the question ask? It asks, "What does fear *look like*?" Now look at the purpose question: "How does this speaker *picture* fear?" These two questions are very much alike. The purpose question will not always be similar to the test questions, however. Remember, the main point of the purpose question is to help you focus your reading.

TEST-TAKING HINTS

- **Read the purpose question.** As you begin to read a selection, focus your attention on what the purpose question asks.
- **Find the line number.** Every fifth line will have a number next to it.

PURPOSE QUESTIONS AND LINE NUMBERS

Questions 1 and 2 are based on the passage below. Read the purpose question, and think about it as you read the passage.

HOW DOES THIS MOTHER ENCOURAGE HER SON?

Well, son, I'll tell you:
Life for me ain't been no crystal stair.
It's had tacks in it,
And splinters,
5 And boards torn up,
And places with no carpet on the floor—
Bare.
But all the time
I'se been a-climbin' on,
10 And reachin' landin's,
And turnin' corners,
And sometimes goin' in the dark
Where there ain't been no light.
So, boy, don't you turn back.
15 Don't you set down on the steps
'Cause you finds it's kinder hard.
Don't you fall now—
For I'se still goin', honey,
I'se still climbin',
20 And life for me ain't been no crystal stair.

"Mother to Son"
By Langston Hughes

1. In what line does the speaker first compare her life to a stair?
   - **(1)** line 1
   - **(2)** line 2
   - **(3)** line 3
   - **(4)** line 5
   - **(5)** line 20

2. What is this poem's tone?
   - **(1)** sad
   - **(2)** angry
   - **(3)** inspirational
   - **(4)** bitter
   - **(5)** humorous

Answers and explanations start on page 111.

Poetry Starters

Anybody can write a poem. Here's one way to start.

EXAMPLE

Line 1: What word or image creates a strong feeling in you?	green grass
Line 2: What does it do (*look, sound, taste, feel,* or *smell*)?	floats on the sea of earth
Line 3: Repeat something, or make a rhyme.	floats up and down with the wind
Line 4: What do you mean? Make a comparison.	Like a cloud rolling across the sky.

Here's the poem based on the starter above:

Green grass
Floats on the sea of earth
Floats up and down with the wind
Like a cloud, rolling across the sky.

Now write your own poem **using** the poetry starter.

Line 1: Write a word or image that creates a strong feeling.
Line 2: Write how it looks, feels, smells, or tastes.
Line 3: Repeat something or make a rhyme.
Line 4: Use a simile or metaphor to make a comparison.

_____

_____

_____

_____

POETRY-WRITING HINTS

■ Start with a strong image. Ask yourself, *What does it look, sound, taste, feel, or smell like?*

■ Repeat something or make a rhyme.

■ Ask yourself, *What is the meaning?* Let the last line write itself after you take a pause.

■ If you get stuck, read what you have written out loud.

See the *Poetry Starter* on page 124.

A. Answer the questions. Choose another image from the one you used on page 70.

Line 1: What word or image creates a strong feeling in you?	
Line 2: What does it do (*look, sound, taste, feel,* or *smell*)?	
Line 3: Repeat something, or make a rhyme.	
Line 4: What do you mean? Make a comparison.	

Line 1: What word or image creates a strong feeling in you?

_____

Line 2: What does it look, sound, taste, feel, or smell like?

_____

Line 3: Repeat something. Make a rhythm.

_____

Line 4: Make a rhyme.

_____

Line 5: Have your speaker say something.

" _____ "

Line 6: What do you mean? Read aloud. Then let the last line write itself.

_____

B. In a journal, write one or two stanzas from your answers above.

C. Self-Check List

How did you like writing this poem? _____

_____

Did you think it was something you would do again? _____

Did you learn something? What? _____

_____

Which part of the poetry starter, or which hint on page 70, was the most helpful to you? Why? _____

_____

Answers and explanations start on page 112.

GED Review: Poetry

Choose the <u>one best answer</u> to the questions below.

<u>Questions 1 through 5</u> refer to the following poem.

HOW DOES THIS PERSON THINK ABOUT A SQUIRREL IN THE ROAD?

It is what he does not know,
Crossing the road under the
    elm trees,
About the mechanism of my car,
About the Commonwealth of
    Massachusetts,
5 About Mozart, India, Arcturus,

That wins my praise. I engage
At once in whirling squirrel-praise.

He obeys the orders of nature
Without knowing them.
10 It is what he does not know
That makes him beautiful.
Such a knot of little purposeful
    nature!

I who can see him as he cannot
    see himself
Repose in the ignorance that is
    his blessing.

15 It is what man does not know
    of God
Composes the visible poem of
    the world.
        . . . Just missed him!

"On a Squirrel Crossing the Road
in Autumn, in New England"
By Richard Eberhart

1. What is the speaker doing?
   (1) driving
   (2) crossing a road
   (3) writing a traffic ticket
   (4) obeying nature's orders
   (5) composing a poem

2. In Line 12, Eberhart compares the squirrel to which of the following?
   (1) a man
   (2) a knot
   (3) the car
   (4) Massachusetts
   (5) elm trees

3. What is the tone of the poem?
   (1) grief
   (2) playfulness
   (3) anger
   (4) weariness
   (5) disgust

4. In which stanza does the phrase "missed him!" appear?
   (1) stanza 1
   (2) stanza 2
   (3) stanza 3
   (4) stanza 4
   (5) stanza 5

5. What is the poem's message?
   (1) Squirrels are not very smart.
   (2) Be careful while driving.
   (3) Beauty is in the unknown.
   (4) Squirrels should be eliminated.
   (5) Poems are visible.

Questions 6 through 10 refer to the following poem.

WHAT DOES THIS WOMAN WANT?

like my mother and her grandmother
    before
i paddle around the house
in soft-soled shoes
chasing ghosts from corners
5 with incense
they are such a disturbance my ghosts
they break my bric-a-brac and make
me forget to turn my heating stove

the children say you must come to live
10 with us   all my life i told them i've lived
with you   now i shall live with myself

the grandchildren say it's disgraceful
you in this dark house with the curtains
pulled   snuff dripping from your chin
15 would they be happier if i smoked
    cigarettes

i was very exquisite once   very small
    and well courted
some would say a beauty when my
    hair was plaited
and i was bustled up

my children wanted my life
20 and now they want my death

but i shall pad around my house
in my purple soft-soled shoes
i'm very happy now
it's not so very neat, you know, but it's my
25 life

"Once a Lady Told Me"
By Nikki Giovanni

6. How is the word *life* made powerful at the end of the poem?
   (1) The word is defined.
   (2) It is on a line by itself.
   (3) It rhymes with another word.
   (4) The word is capitalized.
   (5) An exclamation point is added.

7. Which of the following phrases best states the theme of the poem?
   (1) *now I shall live with myself*
   (2) *it's not so very neat*
   (3) *and I was bustled up*
   (4) *now they want my death*
   (5) *grandchildren say it's disgraceful*

8. How many sentences could you make from lines 9 through 11?
   (1) 1
   (2) 2
   (3) 3
   (4) 4
   (5) 5

9. What is the tone of this poem?
   (1) angry
   (2) amused
   (3) shocked
   (4) proud
   (5) sorrowful

10. What does the speaker mean when she says, "Now they want my death?"
    (1) Her children want her to die.
    (2) The speaker wants to die.
    (3) The speaker's children want to die.
    (4) The children want the speaker to give up her freedom.
    (5) The children want to be able to chase the speaker's ghost.

Answers and explanations start on page 112.

Drama

LESSON GOALS

READING SKILLS

- Set the stage
- Picture the characters
- Tell the story

GED TEST-TAKING SKILLS

- Applying ideas to a new situation

READING & WRITING CONNECTION

- Writing a review

GED REVIEW

1. Think About the Topic

About one-fourth of the questions on the GED Reading Test are based on drama. Drama is fiction that was written to be performed. It can be a play, a movie, or a television show. The written form of drama is called a **script.**

In this program, you will be introduced to drama by a teacher and group of GED students who are writing their own plays. You'll also meet two directors and a group of actors rehearsing scenes from a play they are performing.

To help you understand drama, this program will show you the different parts of a play. You will see a GED class read part of a script written by a GED student. You will also see a different part of that same play performed on stage.

2. Prepare to Watch the Video

This program will give you an overview of the components that make up a play: the script, the scenery or setting, the words and actions of the characters, and the problems the characters have to deal with. Think of a play, movie, or television show that you have seen recently, and answer the questions below.

What was the title (the name)? _____

What was the name of a character you liked? _____

Where did most of the action take place? _____

Perhaps you wrote about a TV show like *ER*. *Dr. Carter* is the name of a character, and most of the action takes place in a *hospital emergency room.*

3. Preview the Questions

Read the questions under *Think About the Program,* and keep them in mind as you watch the program. You will review them after you watch.

4. Study the Vocabulary

Review the terms to the right. Understanding the meaning of key drama vocabulary will help you understand the video and the rest of this lesson.

WATCH THE PROGRAM

As you watch the program, pay special attention to the host who introduces or summarizes major drama ideas that you need to learn about. The host will also give you important information about the GED Reading Test.

AFTER YOU WATCH

1. Think About the Program

What are some of the different jobs involved in putting on a play?

What is the purpose of stage directions?

Why is it important to picture the play in your mind?

Why do you need to know a character's motivation?

What are some of the parts of the plot of a play?

2. Make the Connection

The program shows a scene from the play *Consequences,* written by a GED student. What subject might you write a play about? Do you think it would be difficult to write a play? Why or why not?

TERMS

character—a person who **participates in the action** of a play

climax—the moment in the play where the tension is the highest

dialogue—conversation between two or more characters in a play

external conflict— a struggle between two characters or a character and an outside force

internal conflict— a struggle characters have within themselves

motivation—the reason behind a character's actions

plot—the events in the play and the order in which they happen; the story line

scene—the setting of the play that describes what the stage looks like

script—the written play

stage directions— information about what an actor is doing or how the actor is responding; usually in parentheses

theme—the most important idea that the playwright is trying to share

"Scripts are written in a special format that helps actors and directors know what the writer had in mind."

Setting the Stage

Script Format

As you learned in the program, drama starts with a **script,** the written form of the play. Reading the script for a play may seem overwhelming, but knowing the format will help. A script begins with a description of the **scene,** or setting. The setting is what the stage looks like when the curtain goes up—for example, a living room, an army base, or a city street.

The name of each character is followed by that character's **dialogue. Stage directions** are in parentheses and tell the actor how to say the words (angrily, sadly) or how to move around the stage (dancing, running).

EXAMPLE

1965, a high school dance. Folding chairs and streamers. Two sixteen-year-old girls enter. SUSAN, wearing a kilt and button-down sweater. HEIDI wears a traditional shirtwaist. The girls find a corner and look out at the dance floor as they sing and sway to the music. "The Shoop Shoop Song" is playing. "Does he love me? I wanna know. How can I tell if he loves me so?"

SUSAN (*singing*): Is it in his eyes?

HEIDI (*singing*): Oh nooooooo, you'll be deceived.

SUSAN (*singing*): Is it in his eyes?

HEIDI (*singing*): Oh, no, he'll make believe.

SUSAN: Heidi! Heidi! Look at the guy over at the radiator.

From *The Heidi Chronicles*
By Wendy Wasserstein

1. What is the scene, or setting, for this play?_____

Did you say something like, *a high school dance in 1965* or *a dance with two teenage girls who are singing?* If so, you are correct.

2. Which of the following is a stage direction?
   a. (*singing*)
   b. "Look at the guy over at the radiator."

If you answered *a.* (*singing*), you are right. The actors are directed to sing the words.

A. Read the drama passage below. Picture the setting as you read it.

GRACE: *A very light-skinned African-American woman in her late 20's, early 30's. She is thin and rather "slight." She carries a studied "air" of self-conscious "refinement" and speaks with a soft, lilting Tennessee accent. She is dressed in the "dress up" style of the early 1950s. A close-fitting hat is banded around the top of her head,*

5 *perhaps with a bit of a small veil attached. She wears summer net gloves, stockings with the seams down the back, 50's style high heels, a "smart summer suit" of the mass-produced variety based on "high fashion." Her pocket book, which usually dangles from her wrist, is resting in her lap.*

CLARE: *Dark-skinned African-American woman, same age as* GRACE. *Rather hefty with*

10 *a deliberate "commanding" bravado that disguises her vulnerability underneath.*

SETTING: *A "homestyle" diner in Dearborn Heights.*

TIME: *A mid-Summer Day, 1951*

CLARE: *(Fanning her perspiration.)* Whew! If it ain't hot as all-get out, out there. *(Smiling* GRACE *helps* CLARE *with the packages which they tuck underneath their seats.)*

15 GRACE: Oh, you should feel "Knoxville" you think this is aggravating! I thought moving to Michigan was my release from "the fiery furnace," I see I was mistaken . . .

From *Dearborn Heights*
By Cassandra Medley

B. Use the stage directions to answer the questions below.

  I. Where and when does this scene take place? _____

    _____

  2. What are characteristics that Clare and Grace have in common?

    _____

C. Read the dialogue. Choose the correct answer to the question below.

  3. Grace and Clare are talking about _____
    a. the weather   **b.** a furnace

Answers and explanations start on page 113.

Picturing the Scene

As you learned in the program, you can **picture the scene** or setting of a play by reading the first page of the script, where the playwright describes how the scene should look on the stage. Throughout the script, you may find additional stage directions that give information about the scene. For example, the scene may change from a living room to a restaurant or a nightclub. The details the playwright uses to describe the scene make it come alive for the person reading the play.

EXAMPLE

(The time is early fall, 1977. The setting is a gypsy cab station in Pittsburgh, Pennsylvania. The paint is peeling off the walls, and the floor is covered with linoleum that is worn through in several areas. In the middle of the wall stage left sits an old-fashioned pot-bellied stove that dominates the room. Upstage of it is a blackboard on which is written the rates to different parts of the city, and the daily, marginally illegal policy numbers. Next to the blackboard a sign reads "Beckers's Rules: 1. No overcharging; 2. Keep car clean; 3. No drinking; 4. Be courteous; 5. Replace and clean tools." Downstage on the wall is a pay telephone. The entire right wall is made up of the entrance down right and a huge picture window. Along the upstage wall is a sofa, with several chairs of various styles and ages scattered about to complete the setting.

As the scene opens it is mid-morning. YOUNGBLOOD and TURNBO sit facing each other on folding chairs in front of the sofa. They are playing checkers, with the checkerboard on their knees in front of them. FIELDING sits in a chair down left.)

From *Jitney*
By August Wilson

1. Which of the following best describes this cab company?
   a. new and prosperous
   b. run-down and not too busy

Did you say *b*, the cab company is *run-down and not too busy?* If so, you are correct. The details about the worn-out linoleum and the peeling paint make the setting appear run-down. The fact that the two characters are playing checkers means it's not too busy.

2. Based on the actions of Youngblood and Turnbo, which of the following is most likely to be true?
   a. They are angry about not having enough work.
   b. They are passing the time.

If you answered *b*, you are correct. Playing checkers at work means they are passing time until they get a call. There is no evidence that they are upset about a lack of work.

A. Read the drama passage below. Picture the scene as you read it.

A melody is heard, played upon a flute. It is small and fine, telling of grass and trees and the horizon. The curtain rises.

Before us is the Salesman's house. We are aware of towering, angular shapes behind it, surrounding it on all sides. Only the blue light of the sky falls upon the house and forestage;
5 *the surrounding area shows an angry glow of orange. As more light appears, we see a solid vault of apartment houses around the small, fragile-seeming home. An air of the dream clings to the place, a dream rising out of reality. The kitchen at center seems actual enough, for there is a kitchen table with three chairs, and a refrigerator. But no other fixtures are seen. At the back of the kitchen there is a draped entrance, which*
10 *leads to the living room. To the right of the kitchen, on a level raised two feet, is a bedroom furnished only with a brass bedstead and a straight chair. On a shelf over the bed a silver athletic trophy stands. A window opens onto the apartment house at the side.*

Behind the kitchen, on a level raised six and a half feet, is the boys' bedroom, at present barely visible. Two beds are dimly seen, and at the back of the room a dormer window.
15 *(This bedroom is above the unseen living room.) At the left a stairway curves up to it from the kitchen.*

From *Death of a Salesman*
By Arthur Miller

B. Answer the questions about the scene.

  1. What rooms of the house are shown in the scene?

      _____

  2. Which of the following moods is suggested by the "angry glow of orange" light
     (lines 4–5)?
     a. comfort
     b. irritation

C. Choose the best answers for the following questions.

  3. Based on the description of the scene, who most likely lives in this house?
     a. a family
     b. a single person

  4. Based on the description of the scene, what is one thing that we know about
     a character?
     a. Someone is a cook.
     b. Someone is an athlete.

Answers and explanations start on page 113.

Picturing the Characters

Understanding Dialogue

A play's **characters** are the people who are taking part in the action. The conversation between two or more characters is called **dialogue.** Characters in a play say and do things for a reason. The reason behind a character's actions is the person's **motivation.** To figure out the motivation, ask yourself, *What is the character doing? Why? What is the character trying to say or achieve?* Try to *be* the characters in the play. What would motivate you to say and do those things?

EXAMPLE

ELAIN: I don't see why you're so interested in being Miss Firecracker; there's nothing to it.

CARNELLE: Well, not for you. See, Elain was Miss Firecracker way back when she was just eighteen.

ELAIN: Well, seventeen, actually.

CARNELLE: Anyway, it was way back that first year when I came to live with them. She was a vision of beauty riding on that float with a crown on her head waving to everyone. I thought I'd drop dead when she passed by me.

ELAIN: All that was ages ago. It's silly to think about.

CARNELLE: Anyway, I just thought I'd give it a whirl. I'm twenty-four. Twenty-five's the age limit. I just thought I'd give it a whirl while I still could.

From *The Miss Firecracker Contest*
By Beth Henley

1. Does Elain understand why Carnelle wants to be Miss Firecracker? _____

If you answered *no,* then you are correct. In the dialogue, Elain says to Carnelle, "I don't see why you're so interested in being Miss Firecracker . . ."

2. Based on the dialogue, which of the following is Carnelle's motivation, or reason, for wanting to be Miss Firecracker?
    a. She knows she can win.
    b. She would like to feel special and beautiful, like Elain.

If you answered *b,* you are right. Elain talks about how beautiful Carnelle looked when she was Miss Firecracker.

A. Read the drama passage below. Picture the characters as you read it.

RIDGEON: I cant be your friend on false pretences. Something has got me by the throat: the truth must come out. I used that medicine myself on Blenkinsop. It did not make him worse. It is a dangerous medicine: it cured Blenkinsop: it killed Louis Dubedat. When I handle it, it cures. When another man handles
5   it, it kills—sometimes.

JENNIFER (*naively: not yet taking it all in*): Then why did you let Sir Ralph give it to Louis?

RIDGEON: I'm going to tell you. I did it because I was in love with you.

JENNIFER (*innocently surprised*): In lo—You! An elderly man!

RIDGEON (*thunderstruck, raising his fists to heaven*): Dubedat: thou art avenged!
10   (*He drops his hands and collapses on the bench.*) I never thought of that.
        I suppose I appear to you a ridiculous old fogey.

JENNIFER: But surely—I did not mean to offend you, indeed—but you must be at least twenty years older than I am.

RIDGEON: Oh, quite. More, perhaps. In twenty years you will understand how
15   little difference that makes.

JENNIFER: But even so, how could you think that I—his wife—could ever think of you—

RIDGEON (*stopping her with a nervous waving of his fingers*): Yes, yes, yes, yes: I quite understand: you neednt rub it in.

20 JENNIFER: But—oh, it is only dawning on me now—I was so surprised at first—do you dare to tell me that it was to gratify a miserable jealousy that you deliberately—oh! oh! You murdered him.

From *The Doctor's Dilemma*
By George Bernard Shaw

B. Use the dialogue to answer the question below.

    1. What is Ridgeon's reason, or motivation, for murdering Louis Dubedat?

    _____

C. Read the dialogue. Choose the correct answer to the question below.

    2. How does Jennifer respond to Ridgeon's feelings for her?
        a. She is flattered and very interested.
        b. She is surprised because he is much older.

Answers and explanations start on page 113.

Picturing the Action

As you learned in the program, a play includes many events or actions. These events make up the plot. Another way to think of the **plot** is to think of it as the story. What story does the play tell? For example, the plot of *Romeo and Juliet* is that a boy and girl meet, fall in love, and have problems. The problems characters face are the play's **conflict.** Conflict is what moves the plot along. The **climax** occurs when the conflict hits its moment of highest tension. Read the passage below. Try to picture the action.

EXAMPLE

ERNIE: Bigger, get away from here.

BIGGER (*Whirling on him and jerking out his knife.*): Make me!

ERNIE: I'll fix you this time—(*He turns around and reaches up as if to lift a hidden weapon down from above the door. But BIGGER springs forward, grabs him and jerks him out to the sidewalk. With a swipe of his knife he cuts off a piece of ERNIE's coat and holds it up, yelling.*)

BIGGER: This is a sample of the cloth! Wanta see a sample of the flesh?

ERNIE (*Gasping.*): I'll get my gun—I'll shoot you—

G.H.: Come on. Let's get away from here.

From *Native Son*
By Paul Green

1. Explain what Ernie's last action is in this passage.

_____

Did you say something like, *Ernie, gasping for breath, threatens to shoot Bigger?* If so, you are correct.

2. Which of the following is the climax of this excerpt?
    a. Ernie tells Bigger to leave.
    b. Bigger cuts off a piece of Ernie's coat.

If you answered *b,* you are correct. This is the moment of highest tension.

3. Describe the plot of this excerpt.

_____

_____

A possible answer is, *Ernie wants Bigger to leave. Bigger pulls a knife on him. They fight, and Bigger cuts off a piece of Ernie's clothing. Bigger and Ernie threaten to hurt each other more. G.H. wants to leave.*

A. Read the drama passage below. Picture the action as you read it.

AMANDA (*calling*): Tom?—

TOM: Yes, Mother.

AMANDA: We can't say grace until you come to the table!

TOM: Coming, Mother. (*He bows slightly and withdraws, reappearing a few moments*
5   *later in his place at the table.*)

AMANDA (*to her son*): Honey, don't *push* with your *fingers*. If you have to push
      with something, the thing to push with is the crust of the bread. And chew—
      chew! Animals have sections in their stomachs which enable them to digest
      food without mastication, but human beings are supposed to chew their food
10   before they swallow it down. Eat food leisurely, son, and really enjoy it. A
      well-cooked meal has lots of delicate flavors that have to be held in the
      mouth for appreciation. So chew your food and give your salivary glands a
      chance to function!

(*Tom deliberately lays his imaginary fork down and pushes his chair back from the table.*)

15 TOM: I haven't enjoyed one bite of this dinner because of your constant
      directions on how to eat it. It's you that makes me rush through meals with
      your hawklike attention to every bite I take. Sickening—spoils my appetite—
      all this discussion of animals' secretion—salivary glands—mastication!

AMANDA (*lightly*): Temperament like a Metropolitan star! (*He rises and crosses*
20   *downstage.*) You're not excused from the table.

TOM: I am getting a cigarette.

AMANDA: You smoke too much.

From *The Glass Menagerie*
By Tennessee Williams

B. Answer the question about the action of the play.

 1. Which of the following statements best sums up the plot?
    a. Tom joins his mother at dinner, gets fed up with her remarks, and leaves
          to smoke.
    b. Tom comes to dinner angry and immediately upsets his mother.

C. Respond to the following question.

 2. What are two actions that Tom performs during this passage?

Answers and explanations start on page 113.

"I had a little idea about a kid who is materialistic. He wants to have good things, but he doesn't know who he's really hurting."

Telling the Story

External Conflict

You learned in the program that the play *Consequences* is a story about a character whose parents find $4000 in his coat pocket. The son and his parents have an argument about where the money came from. The father pushes the son and asks if he's dealing drugs. This is an example of **external conflict,** a struggle between characters.

What is the important message of this play? It might be that your actions have consequences that affect other people. This important idea that the writer wants to get across is the **theme.** Characters' words and actions can help you identify the theme.

E X A M P L E

> VANDERGELDER (*Loudly*): I tell you for the hundredth time you will never marry my niece.
>
> AMBROSE (*Thirty; dressed as an "artist."*): And I tell you for the thousandth time that I will marry your niece; and right soon, too.
>
> VANDERGELDER: Never!
>
> AMBROSE: Your niece is of age, Mr. Vandergelder. Your niece has consented to marry me. This is a free country, Mr. Vandergelder—not a private kingdom of your own.
>
> VANDERGELDER: There are no free countries for fools, Mr. Kemper. Thank you for the honor of your visit—good morning.
>
> From *The Matchmaker*
> By Thornton Wilder

1. What is Ambrose's conflict with Vandergelder about?

_____

Did you say something like, *Ambrose wants to marry Vandergelder's niece, but Vandergelder won't give his consent?* If so, you are correct.

2. Which of the following statements best summarizes the theme of this excerpt?
   a. Strong feelings of love and family can create heated arguments.
   b. Two men will always fight over who a woman should marry.

Did you answer *a*? If so, you are correct. The conflict in this play is caused by Ambrose's love and Vandergelder's feelings for his family (his niece).

A. Read the drama passage below.

LALLIE: This land been in your family back before anybody can remember, and I don't think you oughta be sellin' it.

JED: You heard him, Lallie—I ain't sellin' the land, I'm just sellin' the mineral rights.

LALLIE: I don't think you oughta be sellin' any part of it, even them rocks.

5 JED: Lallie, I know what I'm doin' here.

JT (*smiling*): I understand your feelings, ma'am, 'bout the land, and as a mountain boy I share 'em, but I don't think any of your family'd begrudge you makin' a livin' off your land. What's important is the *land,* that it *stays* in your family.

LALLIE: That's right, but . . .

10 JT: Now think about it. Everybody knows with corn, couple of bad seasons back to back and you might have to sell a piece of your land—all of it maybe—just to get by. But with all that *money,* folks, that one hundred and seventy-nine dollars, you're covered. You got somethin' to fall back on.

JED: Man's gotta point, Lallie.

15 JT: And why not make your life a little easier right now, Lallie? You know—get a new stove, maybe. A new dress for your daughter. A new—

LALLIE: We don't need things. We got everything we need.

JED: Lallie . . .

From *Tall Tales*
By Robert Schenkkan

B. Write your answer to the question below.

1. Which characters are in conflict with each other?

_____

C. Choose the correct answer to the following question.

2. Which of the following statements shows the conflict between the characters?
   a. "Man's got a point, Lallie."
   b. "I don't think you oughta be sellin' any part of it, even them rocks."

Answers and explanations start on page 113.

Internal Conflict

Have you ever been confused about the right thing to do? Have you ever gone over both sides of an issue in your head? This is a form of **internal conflict.** Internal conflict is the conflict that occurs within a character. A character may struggle with feelings of guilt, fear, or doubt. A character may have an internal conflict over how to deal with an external conflict he or she is facing, or the internal conflict may be the central conflict of the play. To figure out a character's internal conflict, ask, *What is upsetting the character?*

EXAMPLE

> MAY (*very cold, quick, almost monotone voice like she's writing him a letter*): I don't understand my feelings. I really don't. I don't understand how I could hate you so much after so much time. How, no matter how much I'd like to not hate you, I hate you even more. It grows. I can't even see you now. All I see is a picture of you. You and her. I don't even know if the picture's real anymore. I don't even care. It's a made-up picture. It invades my head. The two of you. And this picture stings even more than if I'd actually seen you with her. It cuts me. It cuts me so deep I'll never get over it. And I can't get rid of this picture either. It just comes. Uninvited. Kinda' like a little torture. And I blame you more for this little torture than I do for what you did.
>
> EDDIE (*standing slowly*): I'll go.
>
> MAY: You better.
>
> From *Fool for Love*
> By Sam Shepard

1. Why is May upset?

   _____

Did you say something like, *May has a picture of Eddie with another woman in her mind and can't get rid of it, and she hates Eddie because of it?*

2. Which of the following statements shows that the conflict is internal?
   a. "It's a made-up picture. It invades my head."
   b. "I don't understand how I could hate you so much after so much time."

If you answered *a*, you are right. May struggles more with her *idea* of what happened than she does with what *actually* happened.

3. Is this statement true or false?

   "And I blame you more for this . . ." is an example of internal conflict. _____

The statement is *false*. May is discussing her anger with Eddie, an external conflict.

A. Read the drama passage below.

MAMA: You don't like it here.

JESSIE (*Smiling*): Exactly.

MAMA: I meant here in my house.

JESSIE: I know you did.

MAMA: You never should have moved back in here with me. If you'd kept your little house or found another place when Cecil left you, you'd have made some new friends at least. Had a life to lead. Had your own things around you. Give Ricky a place to come see you. You never should've come here.

JESSIE: Maybe.

MAMA: But I didn't force you, did I?

JESSIE: If it was a mistake, we made it together. You took me in. I appreciate that.

MAMA: You didn't have any business being by yourself right then, but I can see how you might want a place of your own. A grown woman should . . .

JESSIE: Mama . . .I'm just not having a very good time and I don't have any reason to think it'll get anything but worse. I'm tired. I'm hurt. I'm sad. I feel used.

MAMA: Tired of what?

JESSIE: It all.

MAMA: What does that mean?

JESSIE: I can't say it any better.

From '*Night, Mother*
By Marsha Norman

B. Write your answer to the question below.

1. Is Jessie's conflict within herself or with her mother? Explain.

_____

C. Choose the correct answer to the question below.

2. Which of the following statements describes the internal conflict Mama is having?
   a. Mama is worried about Jessie but doesn't know how to help her.
   b. Mama wishes that Jessie would realize she has a decent life.

Answers and explanations start on page 113.

Applying Ideas to a New Situation

On the GED Reading Test, some of the questions will ask you to take an idea from the passage you have just read and apply that idea to a different situation. For example, if a character is bold and outspoken in the passage, you can use that to figure out how that character might act in other situations.

EXAMPLE

> GRACE: Oh, you should feel "Knoxville" if you think this is aggravating! I thought moving to Michigan was my release from "the fiery furnace," I see I was mistaken . . . truth is I done pulled off my shoes ha . . . I'm [*Whispering.*] "in my stocking feet."

From *Dearborn Heights*
By Cassandra Medley

If Grace were a nurse, which of the following would she be most likely to do?
(1) work in her stocking feet
(2) take off her nurse's hat to make herself comfortable
(3) become extremely angry if it was too hot in the hospital
(4) move a patient to a new room without asking her supervisor
(5) be very professional and joyless

The correct answer is **(2) take off her nurse's hat to make herself comfortable.** That answer is correct because Grace makes herself comfortable even though she feels like she may be breaking the rules a bit.

Remember to read each answer choice and look for details such as behaviors or beliefs. Eliminate choices that do not contain details that fit the character.

- **Read each answer choice.** Choice (1) may have seemed correct if you didn't read all the choices.
- **Eliminate choices that do not show the belief or behavior of the character.** Choices (3), (4), and (5) do not reflect Grace's personality. Grace is not angry, rejecting authority, or joyless in the passage.
- **Choose an answer that is consistent with the character.** Choice (2) is similar to Grace making herself more comfortable in the heat; she takes her shoes off even if it may be a little risky or improper to do so.

TEST-TAKING HINTS
- Read each answer choice.
- Eliminate choices that do not show the belief or behavior of the character.
- Choose an answer that is consistent with the character.

Applying Ideas to a New Situation

MAY: ... I don't understand how I could hate you so much after so much time. How, no matter how much I'd like to not hate you, I hate you even more. It grows. I can't even see you now. All I see is a picture of you. You and her. I don't even know if the picture's real anymore. I don't even care. It's a made-
5   up picture. It invades my head. The two of you. And this picture stings even more than if I'd actually seen you with her ...

From *Fool for Love*
By Sam Shepard

Which of the following would May do if she were in a car accident?
(1) exchange insurance information and forget about it
(2) talk with the other driver clearly and without emotion
(3) listen while the other driver yelled at her
(4) go over the accident constantly in her mind
(5) become angry and violent toward the other driver

After reading each choice, you can eliminate options (1), (2), and (3) because these behaviors are not like May's character. Although May might be angry, there is no evidence that she would become violent, so you can eliminate option (5). Option **(4) go over the accident constantly in her mind** is similar to May's behavior in the passage.

GED TEST-TAKING SKILL PRACTICE

APPLYING TO A NEW SITUATION

Questions 1 and 2 are based on the passage below.

MAMA: ... Child, when do you think is the time to love somebody the most; when they done good and made things easy for everybody? Well then, you ain't through learning—because that ain't the time at all. It's when he's at his lowest and can't believe in hisself 'cause the world done whipped him so. When you
5   starts measuring somebody, measure him right, child, measure him right. Make sure you done taken into account what hills and valleys he come through before he got to wherever he is.

From *A Raisin in the Sun*
By Lorraine Hansberry

1. What would Mama most likely do if she met a homeless woman in the street?
    (1) call the police
    (2) help her buy a cup of coffee
    (3) ignore and walk past her
    (4) give her a long, uplifting speech
    (5) tell her to stop being lazy

2. If Mama were meeting a man for the first time, what would she most likely do?
    (1) act rudely toward him
    (2) like him, no matter what
    (3) judge him on his appearance
    (4) find out as much about him as possible
    (5) like him only if he were successful

Answers and explanations start on page 113.

Writing a Review

You can use what you have learned about reading drama to write your own review of a movie, TV show, or play. You can use questions like the ones below to help you remember the information you will need to start writing your review.

Topic

Write a review about a movie, TV show, or play that you have seen recently. Use the questions below to make notes before you write the review.

What is the title?

My Big Fat Greek Wedding

What was the plot?

A young, unattractive girl who is looking to do more with her life gets a new job and falls in love.

What was the conflict, and how was it resolved?

The man she falls in love with is not Greek. This upsets her traditional Greek family. The characters learn to live with the differences and end up married.

Did you like it or dislike it? Why?

I liked it. It was very funny. It wasn't offensive to Greek culture, and it had a happy ending. I would recommend it.

Here is a sample review based on the notes above.

My Big Fat Greek Wedding is a romantic comedy that will offend no one and will get a few laughs from almost everyone.

The main character starts out as an unattractive young woman working in her family's Greek restaurant. She needs a life. She begins taking a computer class and then goes to work in her aunt's travel agency, where she meets a non-Greek man. This causes problems with her very traditional Greek family. It all works out well in the end, however, and they marry.

This movie creates a joyful sense around Greek culture, and the fun that is gently poked is really more about the conflict between parents and children.

I highly recommend this entertaining movie, which will keep you laughing.

REVIEW-WRITING HINTS

- Name the movie, show, or play, and tell why you liked (or didn't like) it.
- Briefly tell what the plot of the movie is. Be objective.
- Explain an important point about the characters or plot that you liked or disliked.
- Sum up your overall point of view.

A. Reread the writing topic on page 90. Use the questions below to help you write a review.

What is the title of a movie, TV show, or play that you have recently seen?

_____

What was the plot?

_____

_____

What was the conflict, and how was it resolved?

_____

_____

Did you like it or dislike it? Why?

_____

_____

B. On another piece of paper, write a one- or two-paragraph review.

C. Self-Check Questions

Did the writing topic questions help you to write about the movie? Explain.

_____

_____

Did you find it difficult to write any particular part of the review? Explain.

_____

_____

What part of your planning was most helpful to you as you wrote your review? Explain.

_____

_____

Answers and explanations start on page 113.

GED Review: Drama

Choose the <u>one best answer</u> to the questions below.

Questions 1 through 4 refer to the following selection.

HOW DID THIS MAN LIVE HIS LIFE?

Miss Loula: . . . he is dying not owning his own home . . . leaving nothing to you.

Rosa: He always said, "I believe in
5   investin' my money in livin' things. I believe in helpin' the poor an' the unfortunate. Not in storin' money up in banks." . . .

Miss Loula: He did. He did. And he
10   lived by what he believed. There was never less than twelve or fourteen at his table. It was always set, day or night. Set for kin and stranger, rich or poor . . .

15 Rosa: Yes ma'm. He believed in investin' in livin' things.

Miss Loula: Where are these livin' things now? Now that they have a chance to repay him for some of
20   that kindness. Where are the nieces and the nephews and the cousins, or even his sons, Rosa? . . .

Rosa: Well, Miss Loula . . .

Miss Loula: No. They should be here,
25   Rosa. Your brothers should have been here last night. You would have come to them right away, not lettin' twelve hours pass. The brothers are late and the cousins
30   and the nieces and the nephews send their regrets, other responsibilities. Well, I'm writing

them all letters tellin' them exactly what I think.
35   (*A pause. Again she whispers.*)

Rosa, I hate to be frank. But what in the world is going to become of you? If . . .

(Rosa *turns her head away in pain.*)

From *The Death of the Old Man*
By Horton Foote

1. Why does Loula whisper her last line?
    (1) She does not want anyone else to hear.
    (2) She is hoarse from talking so much.
    (3) She is discussing a delicate issue.
    (4) She is trying to frighten Rosa.
    (5) She's ashamed of what she says.

2. What does the dialogue "I believe in investin' my money in livin' things" (lines 4–5) tell us about the dying man?
    (1) He is very generous.
    (2) He is very frivolous.
    (3) He wanted to leave Rosa with nothing.
    (4) He was extremely selfish.
    (5) He believed his house was worthless.

3. Which of following is most likely to happen if the brothers show up?
    (1) Loula gets angry at them.
    (2) Rosa ignores them.
    (3) They apologize for being late.
    (4) They refuse to talk with Rosa.
    (5) They cry about the dying man.

4. What is the conflict in this scene?
    (1) Loula is in conflict with herself.
    (2) Loula is in conflict with Rosa.
    (3) Loula is in conflict with the family.
    (4) Rosa is in conflict with herself.
    (5) The dying man is in conflict with Rosa.

Questions 5 through 8 refer to the following selection.

WHY IS NORA UNHAPPY?

HELMER: You mean I should constantly go and involve you in problems you couldn't possibly help me with?

NORA: I'm not talking of problems. I'm
5 saying that we've never sat down seriously together and tried to get to the bottom of anything.

HELMER: But dearest, what good would that ever do you?

10 NORA: That's the point right there: you've never understood me. I've been wronged greatly, Torvald— first by Papa, and then by you.

HELMER: What! By us—the two
15 people who've loved you more than anyone else?

NORA (*shaking her head*): You never loved me. You've thought it fun to be in love with me, that's all.

20 HELMER: Nora, what a thing to say!

NORA: Yes, it's true now, Torvald. When I lived at home with Papa, he told me all his opinions, so I had the same ones too; or if they
25 were different I hid them, since he wouldn't have cared for that. He used to call me his doll-child, and he played with me the way I played with my dolls. Then I came
30 into your house—

HELMER: How can you speak of our marriage like that?

NORA (*unperturbed*): I mean, then I went from Papa's hands into
35 yours. You arranged everything to your own taste, and so I got the same taste as you—or I pretended

40 to; I can't remember. I guess a little of both, first one, then the other. Now when I look back, it seems as if I'd lived here like a beggar—just from hand to mouth. I've lived by doing tricks for you, Torvald. But that's the way you wanted it.

From *A Doll House*
By Henrik Ibsen

5. What do the stage directions suggest about Nora's reaction to Helmer?
   (1) She is listening patiently.
   (2) She is standing her ground.
   (3) She agrees with some of what he says.
   (4) She knows inside that he is right.
   (5) She is about to become violent.

6. Which of the following best describes what Helmer wants?
   (1) to get revenge
   (2) to change his old ways
   (3) to have children
   (4) to work hard to earn Nora's respect
   (5) to keep things the same

7. What is the theme of this passage?
   (1) Marriage is often followed by divorce.
   (2) You should discuss your problems.
   (3) Marriage can be confining to a woman.
   (4) Men should share their opinions more.
   (5) Marriage is not an equal partnership.

8. What advice would Nora give to a friend who was getting married?
   (1) Make sure to have something blue.
   (2) Always agree with your husband.
   (3) Be sure you have your own ideas.
   (4) Don't have children too quickly.
   (5) Keep your problems to yourself.

Answers and explanations start on page 114.

GED REVIEW

Reading Posttest

The Reading Posttest on the following pages is similar to the GED Reading Test. However, it has only 20 items, in contrast to 40 items on the actual GED Reading Test.

This posttest consists of short nonfiction, fiction, poetry, and drama passages. Each passage is preceded by a "purpose question." This is not the title of the selection; rather, it is a question that has been written to guide your reading of the piece. You should think about the purpose question as you read the selection.

Read the purpose question, read the selection, and answer the multiple-choice questions. You may refer back to the passage whenever you wish.

The purpose of the posttest is to evaluate your skills with reading selections and answering questions based on them. Do not worry if you cannot answer every question or if you get some questions wrong. The posttest will help you identify the types of reading materials and skills that you need to work on.

Directions

1. Read the sample passage and test item on page 95 to become familiar with the test format.
2. Take the test on pages 96 through 103. Read each passage and then choose the best answer to each question.
3. Record your answers on the answer sheet below, using a No. 2 pencil.
4. Check your work against the Answers and Explanations on page 104.
5. Enter your scores in the evaluation chart on page 105.

READING POSTTEST ■ ANSWER SHEET

Name _____   Date _____

Class _____

1. ①②③④⑤   6. ①②③④⑤   11. ①②③④⑤   16. ①②③④⑤
2. ①②③④⑤   7. ①②③④⑤   12. ①②③④⑤   17. ①②③④⑤
3. ①②③④⑤   8. ①②③④⑤   13. ①②③④⑤   18. ①②③④⑤
4. ①②③④⑤   9. ①②③④⑤   14. ①②③④⑤   19. ①②③④⑤
5. ①②③④⑤   10. ①②③④⑤   15. ①②③④⑤   20. ①②③④⑤

Sample Passage and Test Item

The following passage and test item are similar to those you will find on the Reading Posttest. Read the purpose question, the short passage, and the test item. Then go over the answer sheet sample and explanation of why the correct answer is correct.

Question 0 refers to the following passage.

DO YOU WANT TO WRITE A CHILDREN'S BOOK?

Have you ever thought about writing a children's book? Here are some ideas to get you started. First, choose an age group to write for. For example, you may want to write a novel for children ages 8–10. Then read several children's books such as the Harry Potter books and some of the classics. Next, learn from what you read; don't let your ego get in the way. Publishing is a business, and the editors at publishing houses are looking for books that sell. This means staying away from clichés and stereotypes. Nobody wants another children's book about how the bad guy never wins. Your goal is to write a rich, entertaining story for this savvy new generation of kids. And kids are tough critics, so they'd better like the book. Read your story to some kids you know to see how they like it. Then it's the publisher's turn.

0. What is the purpose of this passage?
   The purpose is to
   (1) describe the pitfalls of writing children's books
   (2) explain why most children's books don't sell very well
   (3) guarantee that anyone can write children's books
   (4) give advice on how to write books that children will like
   (5) emphasize that kids won't like books where the bad guy never wins

Marking the Answer Sheet

0. ①②③④⑤

The correct answer is **(4) give advice on how to write books that children will like.** Therefore, answer space (4) is marked on the answer sheet, as shown above. The space should be filled in completely using a No. 2 pencil. If you change your mind about an answer, erase it completely.

Answer and Explanation

0. **(4) give advice on how to write books that children will like** (Comprehension)
   This answer is correct because the author gives several points about how to write a children's book. Other options may be true, but they do not address the purpose of the whole passage.

Choose the <u>one best answer</u> to the questions below.

<u>Questions 1 through 5</u> are based on the nonfiction passage below.

IS MISS MONLUX
A GOOD TEACHER?

And then I saw them.

The daffodils emerged in a corner of my mind all buttery and golden, and the breeze touched my face with the

5 warmth of a baby's kiss. My eyes still closed, I described what I saw and felt, and Miss Monlux, in a tone blending pride and knowledge, said, "You've learned the

10 most important lesson you'll ever learn about writing. You've learned to visualize. Now put on paper what you see in your heart."

I wrote with a passion that has never

15 left, for she had defined for me not only who I was but who I would always be, forever attempting to translate into words what I visualize in my head. In so doing, she altered the

20 course of my life . . . and eliminated a stammer that she never directly addressed. She didn't have to.

Her push, and her lessons in the days that followed, allowed me to

25 overcome a dismal childhood and gave me new tools to pursue a life free of emotional pain and physical violence. I think often of Calla Monlux and the moment she set me traveling on a

30 new path. I see her as though it were yesterday, the small, knowing smile still glowing across the years.

The vision is clear.

From "A Vision of Daffodils"
By Al Martinez

1. Which of the following statements best tells the main idea of the passage?
   (1) Visualizing is a critical part of writing.
   (2) Miss Monlux taught the author to write.
   (3) Miss Monlux changed the author's life.
   (4) The author had an emotionally painful life.
   (5) The author thinks of Miss Monlux as kind.

2. Which of the following details supports the idea that the speaker still thinks of Miss Monlux?
   (1) The daffodils were buttery and golden.
   (2) Miss Monlux was proud of him.
   (3) Miss Monlux helped him overcome a dismal childhood.
   (4) Miss Monlux gave him more lessons in the following days.
   (5) He still sees Miss Monlux's knowing smile.

3. With which of the following statements would Miss Monlux agree the most strongly?
   (1) Every achievement requires a sacrifice.
   (2) People rarely get ahead in life.
   (3) A watched pot never boils.
   (4) Being sure of yourself is foolish.
   (5) Love and time can make a difference in a life.

4. Which of the following statements is a fact, rather than an opinion?
   (1) Miss Monlux is the best teacher there is.
   (2) The wind always feels like a baby's kiss
   (3) Visualizing is the most important part of writing.
   (4) Writing helped the speaker overcome a dismal childhood.
   (5) Miss Monlux had a beautiful smile.

5. How are the author and Miss Monlux alike?
   (1) They are both sensitive.
   (2) They are both a little peculiar.
   (3) They both are teachers.
   (4) They both suffer from stuttering.
   (5) They both write about daffodils.

Questions 6 through 10 are based on the story below.

DO THE TWINS LIKE THE *GOLDILOCKS* STORY?

"I read a story once," said Cathy soundin like Granny teacher. "About this lady Goldilocks who barged into a house that wasn't even hers. And not

5 invited, you understand. Messed over the people's groceries and broke up the people's furniture. Had the nerve to sleep in the folks' bed."

"Then what happened?" asked Tyrone.

10 "What they do, the folks, when they come in to all this mess?"

"Did they make her pay for it?" asked Terry, makin a fist. "I'd've made her pay me."

15 I didn't even ask. I could see Cathy actress was very likely to just walk away and leave us in mystery about this story which I heard was about some bears.

20 "Did they throw her out?" asked Tyrone, like his father sounds when he's bein extra nasty-plus to the washin-machine man.

"Woulda," said Terry. "I woulda gone
25 upside her head with my fist and—"

"You woulda done whatcha always do—go cry to Mama, you big baby," said Tyrone. So naturally Terry starts
30 hittin on Tyrone, and next thing you know they ramblin [rolling] out the tire and rollin on the ground. But Granny didn't say a thing or send the twins home or step out on the steps
35 to tell us about how we can't afford to be fightin amongst ourselves. She didn't say nuthin. So I get into the tire to take my turn. And I could see her leanin up against the pantry table,
40 starin at the cakes she was puttin up for the Christmas sale, mumblin real low and grumpy and holdin her forehead like it wanted to fall off and mess up the rum cakes.

From "Blues Ain't No Mockin' Bird"
By Toni Cade Bambara

6. Which one of the following events occurred after the twins rolled out of the tire?

   (1) Cathy told the story about Goldilocks.

   (2) Tyrone and Terry asked what happened at the end of the story.

   (3) Tyrone and Terry said what they would have done if they had been in the story.

   (4) Terry started hitting Tyrone.

   (5) Granny started holding her forehead like it wanted to fall off.

7. What would Tyrone and Terry <u>most likely</u> do if they both wanted the last piece of pizza?

   (1) listen to Granny's opinion

   (2) split the piece in half

   (3) ask Cathy to decide who gets the pizza

   (4) go outside and play on the tire

   (5) punch each other and argue

8. What can be inferred about the narrator?
   She is

   (1) a younger sibling

   (2) as feisty as the twins

   (3) thoughtful and observant

   (4) envious of Cathy

   (5) resentful toward the twins

9. Which of the following best describes Granny?

   (1) uninterested in the children

   (2) clueless and silent

   (3) accepting and good-natured

   (4) quiet and upset

   (5) mysterious and kind

10. One reviewer noted that in Bambera's stories, actions speak louder than words. Based on this information and the passage above, which of the following actions says the most about a character and what he or she is feeling?

    (1) Cathy doesn't finish the story.

    (2) The twins ride on the tire.

    (3) Cathy takes her turn on the tire.

    (4) Granny holds her forehead.

    (5) Granny bakes rum cakes.

Questions 11 through 15 are based on the poem below.

WHY DO BOTTLES HAVE NECKS?

What happened is, we grew lonely
living among the things;
so we gave the clock a face,
the chair a back,
5   the table four stout legs
which will never suffer fatigue.

We fitted our shoes with tongues
as smooth as our own
and hung tongues inside bells
10   so we could listen
to their emotional language,

and because we loved graceful profiles
the pitcher received a lip,
the bottle a long, slender neck.

15   Even what was beyond us
was recast in our image;
we gave the country a heart,
the storm an eye,
the cave a mouth
20   so we could pass into safety.

"Things"
By Lisel Mueller

11. What idea from the poem is supported by all the details given about objects with human characteristics?
    (1) Caves' mouths are safe.
    (2) Some things are beyond us.
    (3) We gave objects human characteristics to feel less lonely.
    (4) You can find many things around your house that have human characteristics.
    (5) Objects have feelings, too.

12. Which of the following sets up the rhythm of the poem?
    (1) short lines with simple words
    (2) simple words and long lines
    (3) repeating words and sounds
    (4) referring to objects in our homes
    (5) omitting punctuation

13. What is the poet's purpose for including the image of the table with four stout legs (lines 5–6)?
    (1) It shows sturdiness that is like untiring muscles.
    (2) It emphasizes that the table is short.
    (3) It shows tables have more legs than we do.
    (4) It shows that the table is not broken.
    (5) It emphasizes that the table is not graceful.

14. Which phrase best describes the mood of the poem?
    (1) anxious and suspenseful
    (2) romantic and passionate
    (3) resigned and beautiful
    (4) lighthearted and playful
    (5) peaceful and melancholy

15. Which of the following best states the theme of the poem?
    (1) People do silly things sometimes.
    (2) Everyday objects bring us peace.
    (3) Meaning can be found in storms and caves.
    (4) Naming things is sad and futile.
    (5) We struggle to feel less lonely in the world.

Questions 16 through 20 are based on the drama passage below.

HOW DOES TONY FEEL ABOUT MARIA?

(Tony and Maria slowly walk forward to meet each other. Slowly, as though in a dream, they drift into the steps of the dance, always looking at each other,
5 *completely lost in each other; unaware of anyone, anyplace, any time, anything but one another.)*

TONY: You're not thinking I'm someone else?

10 MARIA: I know you are not.

TONY: Or that we have met before?

MARIA: I know we have not.

TONY: I felt, I *knew* something-never-before was going to happen, had
15 to happen. But this is—

MARIA (*interrupting*): My hands are cold. (*He takes them in his.*) Yours too. (*He moves her hands to his face.*) So warm. (*She moves his hands to*
20 *her face.*)

TONY: Yours, too.

MARIA: But of course. They are the same.

TONY: It's so much to believe—you're not joking me?

25 MARIA: I have not yet learned how to joke that way. I think now I never will.

(Impulsively, he stops to kiss her hands; then tenderly, innocently, her lips. The music bursts out, the lights flare up, and
30 *Bernardo is upon them in an icy rage.)*

BERNARDO: Go home, "American."

TONY: Slow down, Bernardo.

BERNARDO: Stay away from my sister!

TONY: . . . Sister?

From *West Side Story*
By Arthur Laurents

16. What detail from the stage directions lets you know the mood of the scene has changed?
    (1) Tony and Maria walk slowly forward.
    (2) Tony and Maria begin dancing.
    (3) Maria interrupts Tony.
    (4) Tony moves Maria's hands to her face.
    (5) The music blares, and the lights come up.

17. Why does Tony repeat the word "sister?"
    (1) He didn't hear what Bernardo said.
    (2) He is mocking Bernardo.
    (3) He is surprised to find out that Maria is related to Bernardo.
    (4) He thinks that Bernardo is lying and wants to try to get the truth.
    (5) Maria is Tony's sister as well.

18. What type of music and lighting would probably be used if Tony and Maria decided to meet secretly at a café one night?
    (1) fast, eerie music and colorful light
    (2) quiet melodies and low light
    (3) suspenseful music and bright light
    (4) loud drumming and bright light
    (5) upbeat music and cheerful lighting

19. What is the conflict in this scene?
    (1) Bernardo is mad because Tony is American, and Maria isn't.
    (2) Tony should know Maria is Bernardo's sister.
    (3) Bernardo doesn't think that Maria should be kissing a boy.
    (4) Maria is too controlling for Tony.
    (5) Tony and Maria have different ideas about love.

20. Later in the play, Bernardo kills Tony's best friend in a gang fight. Based on this information and the passage above, what is most likely to happen?
    (1) Bernardo tries to make peace with Tony.
    (2) Tony decides to leave Maria.
    (3) Tony fights back against Bernardo.
    (4) Maria sides with her brother, ignoring Tony.
    (5) Tony tries to forgive Bernardo and calm the situation down.

Answers and explanations start on page 104.

Reading Posttest Answers and Explanations

1. **(3) Miss Monlux changed the author's life.** (Comprehension) The details support the main idea that Miss Monlux changed the author's life. He became a writer because she taught him to visualize: "I wrote with a passion that has never left, for she had defined for me not only who I was but who I would always be . . ."

2. **(5) He still sees Miss Monlux's knowing smile.** (Comprehension) This detail supports the idea that the reader still thinks of Miss Monlux often. He can still see her smile "as though it were yesterday." The other details do not say what the author thinks of.

3. **(5) Love and time can make a difference in a life.** (Application) Miss Monlux offered her time, patience, and kindness as a teacher—not directly addressing the author's stammering but giving him a valuable way to visualize and help words come to him. "Her push and her lessons . . . allowed me to overcome a dismal childhood . . ."

4. **(4) Writing helped the speaker overcome a dismal childhood.** (Analysis) This is the only statement that can be proved. The writer states this fact. All of the other statements are opinions because they cannot be proved.

5. **(1) They are both sensitive.** (Synthesis) Both of them are friendly and warm to each other and have a caring relationship. They both seem like gentle souls. The other options are not supported by the passage.

6. **(5) Granny started holding her forehead like it wanted to fall off.** (Comprehension) If you read the passage carefully, you will see that option (5) is the only event that occurs after the twins roll the tire out.

7. **(5) punch each other and argue** (Application) The twins instigate a fight with each other in the passage and are likely to keep doing so in other situations.

8. **(3) thoughtful and observant** (Analysis) The narrator is aware of Granny's reaction even though Granny doesn't speak. She also notices how people sound and act in comparison with others: "asked Tyrone, like his father sounds . . ."

9. **(4) quiet and upset** (Analysis) Granny doesn't send the twins home. Instead, she is grumpy and holding her forehead as if with a headache or fatigue. It is obvious that she is upset even though she does not say anything.

10. **(4) Granny holds her forehead.** (Synthesis) Although all the actions reveal something about the character, the action by Granny reveals the most. She is clearly upset by the behavior of the children but is too tired to do anything about it. She may be fatigued by having to constantly stop the children's fighting.

11. **(3) We gave objects human characteristics to feel less lonely.** (Comprehension) The poem starts with "we grew lonely living among the things." The rest of the poem gives details of how we have made ourselves feel less lonely by giving human characteristics to everyday objects.

12. **(1) short lines with simple words** (Analysis) The rhythm of the poem is established by the way the poet sets up the poem. She uses very simple words in short lines. This gives the poem a quick, smooth rhythm.

13. **(1) It shows sturdiness that is like untiring muscle.** (Analysis) The table legs "never suffer fatigue" and are stout. This is an image of a very strong, sturdy table.

14. **(5) peaceful and melancholy** (Synthesis) The feeling is almost matter-of-fact: we were lonely, so we gave the chair a back, the table legs, and so on. But there is no relief mentioned, so the melancholy remains.

15. **(5) We struggle to feel less lonely in the world.** (Synthesis) The poem discusses the things that people will do to make themselves feel safe and less lonely.

16. **(5) The music blares, and the lights come up.** (Comprehension) The stage directions indicate that the music gets louder and the lights get brighter. This takes us out of a peaceful, romantic moment into an emotionally charged confrontation.

17. **(3) He is surprised to find out that Maria is related to Bernardo.** (Comprehension) If Tony had known Maria's relation to Bernardo, he probably would not have danced with her. He repeats "sister" out of surprise.

18. **(2) quiet melodies and low light** (Application) A romantic setting would most likely include quiet music and dim lighting, not harsh lighting or brash music.

19. **(1) Bernardo is mad because Tony is American and Bernardo's sister isn't.** (Analysis) Bernardo tells Tony to go home, "*American.*" The word is used as an insult. This shows that Bernardo and his sister are not Americans and that Bernardo does not like Americans.

20. **(5) Tony tries to forgive Bernardo and calm the situation down.** (Synthesis) Tony tells Bernardo to slow down instead of becoming angry. He tries to calm Bernardo's rage and prevent the situation from turning into a fight. It is reasonable to assume that he would behave this way in other circumstances.

Posttest Evaluation Chart

Follow these steps for the most effective use of this chart:

■ Check your answers against the Answers and Explanations on page 104.

■ Use the following chart to circle the questions you answered correctly.

■ Total your correct answers in each row (across) for types of reading materials and each column (down) for thinking skills.

You can use the results to determine which types of reading and skills you need to focus on.

■ The column on the left of the table indicates the KET Pre-GED video program and its corresponding lesson in this workbook.

■ The column headings—*Comprehension, Application, Analysis,* and *Synthesis*—refer to the type of thinking skills needed to answer the questions.

SUBJECT AREAS AND THINKING SKILLS

Program	Comprehension	Application	Analysis	Evaluation	Total for Reading Subjects
7 Nonfiction (pp. 14–33)	1, 2	3	4	5	____/5
8 Fiction (pp. 34–53)	6	7	8, 9	10	____/5
9 Poetry (pp. 54–73)	11		12, 13	14, 15	____/5
10 Drama (pp. 74–93)	16, 17	18	19	20	____/5
Total for Skills	____/6	____/3	____/6	____/5	

Answers and Explanations

PROGRAM 7
NONFICTION

Practice 1 (page 17)

1. **b.** Her mother grew up "without affection or closeness or indulgence."

2. **a.** "but all she got was an orange"

3. **b.** "But they gave her little love."

Practice 2 (page 19)

Answers may vary. Sample answers:

1. His attitude is warm, and he lovingly jokes about the town's drawbacks.

2. They put up fake fronts on the downtown buildings.

3. They stand around and talk.

4. The men don't hide their large stomachs.

5. **a.** You could stand in the middle of the street and not be in the way.

Practice 3 (page 21)

1. Compare

2. Compare

3. Contrast

Answers may vary. Sample answers:

4. Both libraries offer students a quiet place to study, and both have similar layouts on the first two floors.

5. The Memorial Library has two large computer labs, which the Davidson doesn't have. Also, the Memorial lets alumni in, and the Davidson doesn't.

Practice 4 (page 23)

1. **d.** had oatmeal instead

2. **b.** animal seemed eager to get food

3. **c.** felt no pressure in the afternoon

4. **a.** at 5 P.M., still feel good

5. **a.** She will enjoy them more when they come back home.

   b. The children will miss her.

Practice 5 (page 25)

1. greatest

2. perfect

3. gorgeous

4. ridiculous

5. hilarious

6. **F** The review lists Ford as the director and Wayne as an actor.

7. **O** Some might not agree the scene is "funny."

8. **F** This is stated in the review.

9. **F** This is mentioned in the review as Ford's birthplace.

10. **O** Some might not agree she has never been lovelier.

Practice 6 (page 27)

Answers may vary. Sample answers:

1. The tone of the passage is humorous.

2. **kidding** This word helps to demonstrate the humorous tone of the passage.

3. **both Chad *and* Jeremy** The italic *and* helps make it a joke. Besides, a musical duo seems unlikely as assassins. This adds to the overall humorous tone of the passage.

4. **Against** The writer thinks children should not play football because it is too dangerous.

GED Test-Taking Skill (page 29)

1. **(2) fatherhood** The writer says the man and his daughter have a genuine parent-child relationship, and he doesn't want to lose custody of her. All of the other choices are mentioned in the passage, but none of them are the movie's main focus.

2. **(3) *I Am Sam* is a good movie worth seeing.** Option (3) is the best answer. The other options are all mentioned in the passage, but none of them are the main point that the writer is trying to get across.

GED Reading and Writing Connection (page 31)

A. On the 5 *W*s Chart:

❑ Did you include the names of the important people involved in the event?

❑ Did you let your reader know when things happened?

❑ Did you include what happened— the major event or action?

❑ Did you let the reader know where the action happened?

B. In the paragraph(s):

❑ Did you use proper grammar?

❑ Did you have a main **idea**?

❑ Did you support your main idea with details?

❑ Did you use words like *when* and *after* to show time order?

Here are sample answers to **page 31:**

B. My roommate, Suzanne Larkin, passed her GED in March. She lives in her own apartment now because she can earn enough to support herself.

C. The *Who* was easy. The *What* was hard at first until I realized passing the test was what she did to inspire me. I don't know if I needed the *Where,* but it helped me think of what she had now that I wanted— her own apartment. The most important *W* was the *What.*

GED Review: Nonfiction (pages 32–33)

1. **(2) They sold to a big farm corporation.** This information is stated directly in the passage.

2. **(4) Grocery store prices are too high.** Although the passage does say that the farmers sold their produce at a lower cost than the grocery stores, that does not mean grocery store prices are too high. Some people may think they are too high, while others may find them reasonable. This is an opinion, not a fact.

3. **(1) He is imaginative.** The farmer came up with a way to farm that could work in the city. By looking at his creative solution to a problem, you can infer that he is an imaginative person.

4. **(1) Farming in the City** Farming in the city is the main subject of the passage. Other options don't fit: the farmers don't give up; there's no discussion of spinach; they don't go to the country; there is no information on how to grow your own food.

5. **(2) The farmers charge lower prices than the stores.** This is the only statement that contrasts the farmers and the grocery stores. Options (1) and (3) mention only one of the two, and options (4) and (5) compare the two.

6. **(2) The family lived on Tremont Avenue.** This is the only statement that is a fact. The other options are false according to the information in the passage.

7. **(1) positive** Even though the passage is about the hard times the family experienced, it focuses on the positives: how the family got through those times and the love of education that developed in Morrie because of his mother. These facts leave a positive feeling.

8. **(4) the Depression** The passage says the Depression caused his lack of work.

9. **(4) She was proud and strong.** Eva was able to help her family make it through the difficult times of the Depression. She also went to school to improve her English. These details paint the picture of a woman who was strong and proud.

10. **(2) He grew to love education.** The passage says, "His love of education was hatched in his mother's arms."

PROGRAM 8
FICTION

Practice 1 (page 37)
1. **a.** serpents of smoke
2. **b.** worked monotonously up and down
3. **a.** river that ran purple
4. **b.** rattling and trembling
5. It was a town of machinery and tall chimneys

Practice 2 (page 39)
1. **b.** mysterious
2. **b.** The light had an unreal greenish color.
3. Possible answers include: sun rising, favorite island, snowy owl waking up.

Practice 3 (page 41)
1. He mentions the boy's mother, and he calls him a son in the last line.
2. He takes up a book and reads.
3. unnecessary
4. civilized

Practice 4 (page 43)
1. dialogue
2. stern
3. no
4. attractive

Practice 5 (page 45)

1. yes

2. no

3. yes

4. no

5. then

6. **(4)** opened the curtains in the front room

   (3) put it in the refrigerator

   (2) washed the produce

Practice 6 (page 47)

1. **a.** He is fired and faces unemployment.

2. **a.** within a character

Answers may vary. Sample answers:

3. There may be a conflict between Sandy and the man about when he is going to go back to work.

4. She feels sorry to see how anxious he is, but she is angry with him because he refuses to look for work.

GED Test-Taking Skill (page 49)

1. **(3) all in her mind** The fact that John sees no reason for her to be suffering, combined with the fact that John is sensible and only believes what he can see or measure, indicates that there is no physical problem with the narrator. However, she is clearly bothered by something, so it must be a mental problem.

2. **(4) find some sort of creative outlet** Gilman overcame her depression by using her creativity in writing. Since she was suffering from a problem similar to that of the narrator, it would be logical that she would recommend a similar solution.

GED Reading and Writing Connection (page 51)

In the journal entry/story review:

❑ Did you state what you liked or disliked about the story?

❑ Did you say what you liked most—for example, a character, a setting, a conflict?

❑ Did you say what you liked least— for example, not enough action or dull characters?

❑ Did you say what your reaction was to the conflict or conflicts?

In the paragraph(s):

❑ Did you use proper grammar?

❑ Did you have a main idea?

❑ Did you support your main idea with details?

Here is a sample paragraph:

I liked the story's conflict, the one going on inside Sandy. She's got a man sitting on her couch, watching TV indefinitely. I disliked the fact that there was not a real dialogue in this passage. My reaction was sympathy for Sandy.

GED Review: Fiction (pages 52–53)

1. **(3) pitiful** The passage takes place during the Great Depression. Both of the families in the passage are very poor. The man in the passage is forced to beg for food and water for his entire family. The reader feels a great deal of pity and sympathy for the character.

2. **(1) poverty and the man** Option (1) is the only logical choice. Options (2), (3), and (4) are all conflicts with other characters, and option (5) is a conflict that occurs within the man. The man's struggle with his poverty is the only option that includes a conflict with an outside force.

3. **(4) The man turns off the hose.** If you read the passage, you can see that this event happens first among the five choices listed.

4. **(4) Mr. Wordsworth's office** The phrase "on his desk" provides a clue as to the location of the scene. Options (1), (2), and (3) are all in Jerome's imagination, and option (5) is not mentioned in the story.

5. **(4) someone outside the story** The characters are referred to by name. No one uses "I." This is a sign that someone outside the story is narrating.

6. **(2) what he thinks** Jerome is very quiet in this passage and doesn't react very much. The only way we can tell what is going on with Jerome is through his thoughts, which reveal a great deal about his character.

PROGRAM 9 POETRY

Practice 1 (page 57)

1. It was a picture I had after the war.

   A bombed English church.

   I was too young to know the word
   English or *war,* but I knew the picture.

2. 13 complete ideas

   It was a picture I had after the war. /

   A bombed English church. / I was
   too young

   to know the word *English* or *war,*

   but I knew the picture. /

   The ruined city still seemed noble. /

   The cathedral with its roof blown off

   was not less godly. / The church was
   the same

   plus rain and sky. / Birds flew in and out

   of the holes God's fist made in the walls. /

   All our desire for love or children

   is treated like rags by the enemy. /

   I knew so much and sang anyway. /

   Like a bird who will sing until

   it is brought down. / When they take

   away the trees, the child picks up a stick

   and says, this is a tree, this the house

   and the family. / As we might. / Through
   a door

   of what had been a house, into the field

   of rubble, walks a single lamb, tilting

   its head, curious, unafraid, hungry. /

Sample answers:

3. The enemy has destroyed our desire for a good life.

4. Even with the bombing, I had hope.

Practice 2 (page 59)

1. three

2. The wind

3. four

4. two

5. I rock my son.

6. **b.** a mother

7. **b.**

8. **c.**

9. **a.**

Practice 3 (page 61)

1. wings, line 8

2. core, line 12

3. I will arise and go now

4. peace

5. I hear

6. yes

Practice 4 (page 63)

1. **c.** desperation

2. **a.** ambition

3. **b.** anger

4. neighborhood

5. lint

Practice 5 (page 65)

1. The boy knows he's hurting his mother again just as his father hurt his mother, but he believes he's doing what men have to do.

2. **b.** grief

3. **Answers may vary. Possible answers include:** gone, whisper, crying, could not feel, and leaving.

Practice 6 (page 67)

1. **b.** secretive

2. **a.** take responsibility in life.

3. **Sample answer:** The speaker wishes to stay in the peace of nature, but he has responsibilities somewhere else.

4. **Sample answer:** In the first stanza, the speaker is secretive and wants to simply sit and watch the snow fall in the woods. In the last stanza, the speaker realizes he cannot put off his responsibilities. This change helps create the theme of growing up and taking responsibility.

5. **Sample answer:** The overall message of the poem seems to be taking responsibility in life. The speaker has things he would like to do, but he says he has made promises to other people, and those have to come first.

GED Test-Taking Skill (page 69)

1. **(2) line 2** This is the best option. Although the other lines mentioned do make comparisons between the speaker's life and a stair, the first such comparison comes in line 2.

2. **(3) inspirational** The speaker in the poem talks about how hard her life has been, but she is not bitter about it. She says she has kept going, and she encourages her son to do the same. The poem is uplifting.

GED Reading and Writing Connection (page 71)

❑ Did you give an image or a feeling in line 1?

❑ Did you give it a look, sound, taste, feeling, or smell in line 2?

❑ Did you repeat something or make a rhythm in line 3?

❑ Did you make a rhyme at the end of line 4 or within line 4?

❑ Did your speaker say something in line 6?

❑ Does line 6 give the theme, or meaning, of your poem?

B. **Answers may vary. Sample poem:**

Restless

Tiny, hard, shooting

Tiny, hard, shooting

HOOOTING HOOTING

I'm a hooting owl.

GED Review: Poetry (pages 72–73)

1. **(1) driving** Although this is not directly stated, the speaker gives certain clues about his activities. He mentions that the squirrel doesn't know about the mechanism of his car, and the last line "Just missed him!" implies that he is driving.

2. **(2) a knot** The speaker says the squirrel is "a knot of little purposeful nature!"

3. **(2) playfulness** The playful tone of this poem is best demonstrated in the last line.

4. **(5) stanza 5** This is the last line of the poem. It therefore occurs in the last stanza. If you count the number of stanzas in the poem, you will come up with five.

5. **(3) Beauty is in the unknown.** The speaker admires the squirrel for the things it doesn't know. He also reflects on what man does not know and realizes it is these things that make the world beautiful.

6. **(2) It is on a line by itself.** Placing the word *life* on a line by itself makes it stand out more and makes its meaning more powerful.

7. **(1) now I shall live with myself** This is the message that the speaker is trying to get across. She wants to continue living by herself, even if others don't feel her life is worth living.

8. **(3) 3** When you read these three lines, you can see that there are three separate thoughts. Therefore, there should be three separate sentences. There should be a period after the words *us, you*, and *myself*. The spaces in the poem symbolize the end of a sentence.

9. **(4) proud** The speaker in this poem will not take help from her children and refuses to live with anyone else. She wants to live on her own and take care of herself. She is too proud to depend on anyone else.

10. **(4) The children want the speaker to give up her freedom.** This is not a literal statement. The speaker is speaking figuratively. Her children do not want her to actually die. They want her to come live with one of them. However, giving up her personal freedom and depending on someone else to take care of her is a type of "death" for the speaker.

PROGRAM 10
DRAMA

Practice 1 (page 77)

1. The scene takes place in a homestyle diner in Dearborn Heights, on a summer day in 1951.

2. Clare and Grace are both African-American women of the same age.

3. **a.** the weather

Practice 2 (page 79)

1. **kitchen and two bedrooms** The living room is mentioned but is described as "unseen" in line 15.

2. **b.** irritation

3. **a.** a family

4. **b.** Someone is an athlete.

Practice 3 (page 81)

1. He is in love with Jennifer, Dubedat's wife.

2. **b.** She is surprised because he is much older.

Practice 4 (page 83)

1. **a.** Tom joins his mother at dinner, gets fed up with her remarks, and leaves to smoke.

2. **Answers will vary. Sample answer:** He bows; he takes his seat at the table; he lays down his fork; he pushes his chair back from the table; he rises and walks across the stage.

Practice 5 (page 85)

1. Jed is in conflict with Lallie and JT over whether or not to sell the mineral rights.

2. **b.** I don't think you oughta be sellin' any part of it, even them rocks.

Practice 6 (page 87)

1. **Answers will vary slightly. Sample answer:** Her conflict is within herself. She is tired and unhappy but not upset with her mother about it.

2. **a.** Mama is worried about Jessie but doesn't know how to help her.

GED Test-Taking Skill (page 89)

1. **(2) She would help her buy a cup of coffee.** In the passage, it's clear that Mama believes it's important to love people even when they are down. So she would most likely make a kind gesture toward the homeless woman.

2. **(4) find out as much about him as possible** In the passage, Mama talks about how important it is to know where someone has come from before you make judgments about the person. So Mama would most likely find out all she could about someone before deciding whether she like the person. She would not make judgments based on the person's looks or level of success.

Reading and Writing Connection (page 91)

A. While answering the questions:

❑ Did you include the name of the movie?

❑ Did you give a brief, objective overview of the plot?

❑ Did you identify the conflict and how it was solved?

❑ Did you include examples of what you liked or disliked about the film?

B. In the paragraphs:

- ❑ Did you include the movie title and why you liked the movie?

- ❑ Did you include a short paragraph about the plot of the movie and discuss the conflict and resolution?

- ❑ Did you write your opinion on an important part of the movie you liked or disliked, such as a character or part of the plot?

- ❑ Did you sum up your opinion? Did you recommend this movie to a friend and explain why or why not?

GED Review: Drama (pages 92–93)

1. **(3) She is discussing a delicate issue.** The stage direction *"Again she whispers"* is followed by a frank statement that is a sensitive matter: What is going to happen to Rosa now that she has been left on her own with no house or money? There is no evidence in the passage to support the other options.

2. **(1) He is very generous.** This statement makes the point that the man gave his time and money to people and didn't just save his money in a bank. There is no evidence to support that he is selfish or frivolous.

3. **(1) Loula gets angry at them.** Loula says the brothers should have been there last night and she will write them to tell them what she thinks. Although they might apologize for being late, there is no information about this in the passage. There is no evidence to support the other options.

4. **(3) Loula is in conflict with the family.** The bulk of Loula's dialogue is about her anger at the family not showing up. She believes they should be there to help Rosa. This is an external conflict. The other options are not supported by the passage.

5. **(2) She is standing her ground.** The stage directions show that Nora is shaking her head in disagreement with Helmer and that she is *"unperturbed."* Although it may seem that she is listening patiently, her dialogue also indicates that she is not backing down from her viewpoint.

6. **(5) to keep things the same** Helmer says he has loved her and can't believe she is speaking of the marriage in such a negative way. There is no indication that he wants revenge, wants to change in response to Nora's concerns, make any additional effort, or have children. He wants things to go on the way they have been. He sees no problems and doesn't understand why Nora is so upset.

7. **(3) Marriage can be confining to a woman.** Nora's dialogue consistently expresses that she has felt trapped and like a doll or child, without room to have her own ideas and opinions: "You arranged everything to your own taste, and so I got the same taste as you . . ."

8. **(3) Be sure you have you own ideas.** Nora is upset because she feels confined in her marriage and as if she does not have an identity of her own. Using this information, it is logical to assume that she would advise a friend who is getting married to be sure to maintain an identity of her own.

Reading Resources

Main Idea and Details Cluster Diagram

You can make a cluster diagram when you are reading for main ideas and details. The **cluster diagram** below shows how one reader outlines the main idea and details for this paragraph about biographies.

> Biographies make history fun to learn. Most biographies contain facts about interesting personalities. They also follow that person's life all the way through. As I get familiar with the person, I get more and more interested in finding out what happened to him or her.

First, she writes the main idea in the center circle. The main idea is the central thought of the paragraph. From that circle, she draws lines out to each detail that supports the main idea.

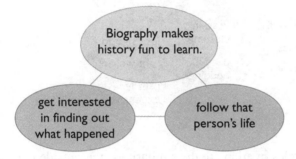

As you see, the detail circles can connect to each other when the details are related.

Try your own cluster diagram to show the main idea and details in the following paragraph.

> Children and pets seem to go together. Most kids beg for a pet at least once before they grow up. If they can't have one at home, they'll befriend someone else's. Or they'll just daydream about getting one. They'll name it, find out what kind of food it likes, plan ways to train it, and make it an imaginary friend.

The main idea and the first detail are done for you.

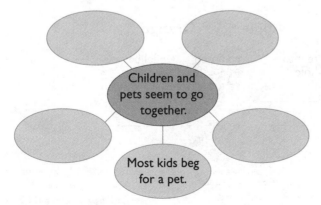

Cluster diagrams are referred to on page 16.

Compare and Contrast Venn Diagram

You can use a **Venn diagram to organize similarities and differences as you read.** The **Venn diagram** shows how one reader compares and contrasts cotton and synthetic fabric.

Both cotton and synthetic fibers are used in clothing and bedding. Cotton fabric usually wears better than synthetic fiber. Many people think it is more comfortable because it "breathes," lets in air and lets out sweat. Cotton does wrinkle, though. Synthetic fiber doesn't wrinkle easily. It looks good, and it is lightweight, so it flatters your shape. It's usually less expensive than cotton.

First, the reader draws two circles that overlap. Then he writes *Cotton* over one and *Synthetic* over the other.

Cotton   **Synthetic**

wears well

breathes

wrinkles

used in clothing

used in bedding

easy to care for

looks good

light weight

usually less expensive

As you see, where the circles overlap are the similarities; the outside parts of the circles show the differences.

Try your own Venn diagram to compare and contrast oranges and apples.

There's an old expression, "It's like comparing apples and oranges." Both are common fruits. Both are handheld. Both are juicy. Here are some differences. You can bite right into an apple, but an orange has to be peeled or sliced. An apple has a white center, but an orange is orange in the middle. Apples are good for pie, and oranges are good for juice.

The first one in each section is done for you.

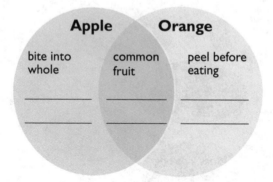

Apple   **Orange**

bite into whole

common fruit

peel before eating

_____   _____   _____

_____   _____   _____

Venn diagrams are referred to on page 20.

Cause-and Effect Chain

You can use a cause-and-effect chain to organize causes and effects while you read. The **cause-and-effect chain** below shows how one reader showed the causes and effects in the paragraph below.

> Because my bus arrived early, I missed it. I caught the next bus, but I got to work late, so I had to work through lunch. This made me grumpy, and unfortunately, I snapped at my boss. He fired me on the spot; that's why I finally joined the circus.

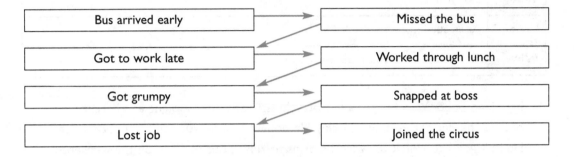

As you see, each effect becomes a cause of another event.

Try your own cause-and-effect chain to show the causes and effects in the paragraph below.

> [President John F. Kennedy] was assassinated, and the government set up the Warren Commission to investigate. They found that Lee Harvey Oswald killed the President by himself. Lee Oswald was murdered by Jack Ruby a few days after the assassination. Jack Ruby had criminal connections. There was no trial for Oswald. He couldn't be questioned. Many suspicious Americans believed they had been fooled.

The first cause and effect are done for you.

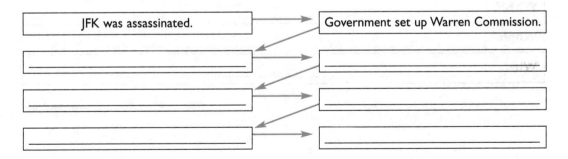

Cause-and-Effect Chains are referred to on page 22.

5 Ws Chart

You can use a 5 *W*s chart to organize facts while you read or to plan something that you will write. Look at how one student, Nate Barlow, uses the 5 *W*s Chart to plan a story about a friend of his.

Who?	Bobby Voils
What?	Bought a Harley
When?	Last year
Where?	At an auction
Why?	To ride out of town on the weekends

My friend Bobby Voils bought a motorcycle last year. After looking at different types of bikes, he decided to buy a Harley. He bought it at an auction for a good price. He isn't going to ride it to work; he plans to ride it out of town on the weekends.

As you see, the 5 *W*s helped Nate to get his thoughts organized.

Try your own 5 *W*s Chart with the following paragraph.

Beverly native and Bates women's basketball standout Lauren Dubois had never played at Salem State's Twig Gymnasium until last night. After her performance, she wishes she could come back for more.

The *Who* and *What* are done for you.

Who?	Lauren Dubois
What?	Played for first time at Salem State
When?	
Where?	
Why?	

5 Ws Charts are referred to on page 30.

Sequence Diagram

The **Sequence Diagram** below shows how one reader mapped out what happens in this passage from Wendell Berry's *A World Lost.*

> That afternoon, as soon as I could escape attention, I knew I would go across the field to Fred Brightleaf's. Fred and I would catch Rufus Brightleaf's past-work old draft horse, Prince, and ride him over to the pond for a swim. And after supper, when Grandma and Grandpa would be content just to sit on the front porch in the dark, and you could feel the place growing lonesome for other times, I would drift away down to the little house beside the woods where Dick Watson and Aunt Sarah Jane lived. While the light drained from the sky and night fell I would sit with Dick on the rock steps in front of the door and listen to him tell of the horses and mules and foxhounds he remembered . . . .

As you see, the events are listed in order from left to right. You could also stack the boxes and have the events go from top to bottom.

Fill out this Sequence Diagram to show the sequence of events in the paragraph by Raymond Chandler on page 39. The initiating event has been done for you.

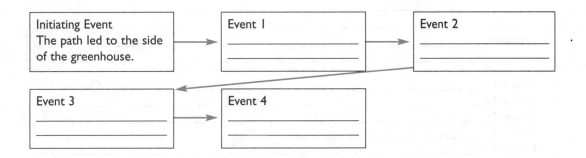

Sequence Diagrams are referred to on page 44.

Story Map

Look at the **Story Map** one student created for the passage on page 46. First she listed the title of the passage. Next she wrote where the passage most likely took place, the setting. Then she listed the characters in the passage. After that she wrote the problem, or conflict, described in the passage. Then she listed the important events that occurred in the passage. Finally she wrote what solution, if any, there was to the conflict.

Title: _Song of Solomon_

Setting: This passage most likely takes place in the living room of a home.

Characters: _Milkman_ _Lena_

Problem: Milkman doesn't want Corinthians to see the man she is dating but can't explain why to Lena

Event 1: _Lena confronts Milkman_
Event 2: _Milkman tries to explain his feeling but can't._
Event 3: _Lena asks Milkman when he started caring about Corinthians_

Solution: There was no solution presented in this passage.

Now create your own Story Map for the passage on page 52. If you don't know the name of a character you may choose to make one up, such as *narrator, man,* or *sister.* The title and the setting have been done for you.

Title: _Grapes of Wrath_

Setting: This passage most likely takes place in front of Mae's house.

Characters: _____ _____ _____
_____ _____

Problem: _____
_____

Event 1: _____
Event 2: _____
Event 3: _____
Event 4: _____
Event 5: _____

Solution: _____
_____

Story Maps are referred to on page 46.

Poetry Starter

This **Poetry Starter** was used to create the poem below.

Line 1 What word or image creates a strong feeling in you?

My new puppy

Line 2 What does it do (*look, sound, taste, feel,* or *smell*)?

Plays and runs

Line 3 Repeat something, or make a rhyme.

Prepares for a nap in the afternoon sun

Line 4 Make a comparison with the image.

Like a toy winding down

Here's the poem based on the starter above:

My new puppy

Plays and runs

Prepares for a nap in the afternoon sun

Like a toy winding down.

Fill out this Poetry Starter to write a poem. Then write a stanza or a whole poem on the lines below.

Line 1 What word or image creates a strong feeling in you?

Line 2 What does it do (*look, sound, taste, feel,* or *smell*)?

Line 3 Repeat something, or make a rhyme.

Line 4 Make a comparison with the image.

Poetry Starters are referred to on page 70.

Credits

READING RESOURCES

page 80, From *The Miss Firecracker Contest* by Beth Henley. © Beth Henley 1985. All inquires should be made to Peter Hagan, The Gersh Agency, 41 Madison Ave., New York, NY 10010. Reprinted with permission.

page 81, From *The Doctor's Dilemma* by Bernard Shaw, 1930. Reprinted by permission of The Society of Authors on behalf of the Bernard Shaw Estate.

page 82, From *Native* Son by Paul Green and Richard Wright, 1941. Reprinted with permission from The Paul Green Foundation.

page 83, From *The Glass Menagerie* by Tennessee Williams, copyright 1945 by Tennessee Williams and Edwina D. Williams; copyright renewed 1973 by Tennessee Williams. Used by permission of Random House, Inc.

page 84, "The Matchmaker" by Thornton Wilder © 1955 The Wilder Family LLC. Reprinted by arrangement with The Wilder Family LLC and The Barbara Hogenson Agency, Inc.

page 85, "Tall Tales", from *The Kentucky Cycle* by Robert Schenkkan, copyright © 1993 by Robert Schenkkan. Used by permission of Plume, an imprint of Penguin Group (USA) Inc.

page 86, *From Fool for Love* by Sam Shepard. © 1983 by Sam Shepard. Reprinted by permission of City Lights Books.

page 87, *Excerpt from Night, Mother: A Play* by Marsha Norman. Copyright © 1983 by Marsha Norman. Reprinted by permission of Hill & Wang, a division of Farrar, Straus and Giroux, LLC.

page 89, From *A Raisin in the Sun* by Lorraine Hansberry, copyright © 1958 by Robert Nemiroff, as an unpublished work. Copyright © 1959, 1966, 1984 by Robert Nemiroff. Used by permission of Random House, Inc.

page 92, From *The Death of the Old Man* © 1955, 1983 by Horton Foote. Reprinted by arrangement with Horton Foote and The Barbara Hogenson Agency, Inc.

page 93, "A Doll House", from *The Complete Major Prose Plays of Henrik Ibsen* by Henrik Ibsen, translated by Rolf Fjelde, copyright © 1965, 1970, 1978 by Rolf Fjelde. Used by permission of Dutton Signet, a division of Penguin Group ((USA) Inc.

page 96, From "A Vision of Daffodils" by Al Martinez from *Modern Maturity,* January/February, 1997. Reprinted by permission of Al Martinez.

page 98, "Blues Ain't No Mockin' Bird" Toni Cade Bambara, *Gorilla, My Love.* New York: Random House, Inc., 1971.

page 100, "Things" Reprinted by permission of Louisana State University Press from *Alive Together: New and Selected Poems* by Lisel Mueller. Copyright © 1996 by Lisel Mueller.

page 102, From *West Side Story* by Arthur Laurents, Stephen Sondheim, Leonard Bernstein, copyright © 1956, 1958 by Arthur Laurents, Leonard Bernstein, Stephen Sondheim and Jerome Robbins. Used by permission of Random House, Inc.